MOON

ZION & BRYCE

JUDY JEWELL & W. C. McRAE

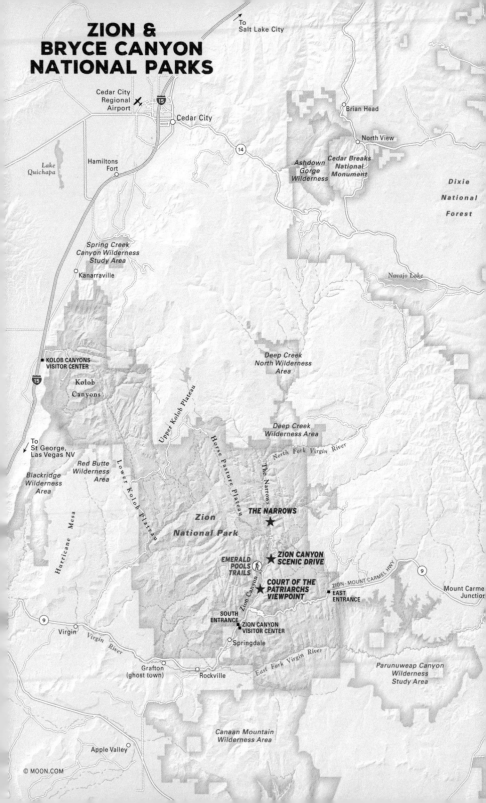

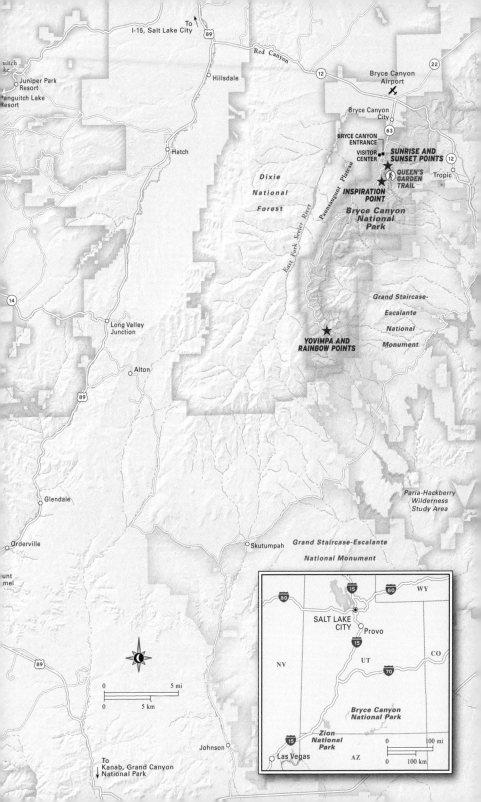

To I-15, Salt Lake City
89

Red Canyon
12

Bryce Canyon Airport
22

Hillsdale

Bryce Canyon City
63

Hatch

BRYCE CANYON ENTRANCE
VISITOR CENTER

SUNRISE AND SUNSET POINTS

12

Tropic

QUEEN'S GARDEN TRAIL

INSPIRATION POINT

Dixie

National

Forest

Paunsaugunt Plateau

Bryce Canyon National Park

East Fork Sevier River

14

Grand Staircase-

Escalante

National

Long Valley Junction

YOVIMPA AND RAINBOW POINTS

Monument

Alton

89

Paria-Hackberry

Wilderness

Study Area

Glendale

Orderville

Skutumpah

Grand Staircase-Escalante

National Monument

unt mel

80

15

80

WY

SALT LAKE CITY

Provo

89

NV

UT

CO

15

70

N

0   5 mi

0   5 km

Bryce Canyon National Park

To Kanab, Grand Canyon National Park

Johnson

15

Las Vegas

Zion National Park

AZ

0   100 mi

0   100 km

CONTENTS

Although every effort was made to make sure the information in this book was accurate when going to press, research was impacted by the COVID-19 pandemic and things may have changed since the time of writing. Be sure to confirm specific details, like opening hours, closures, and travel guidelines and restrictions, when making your travel plans. For more detailed information, see page 150.

Yovimpa Point

WELCOME TO
ZION & BRYCE

FILLED WITH STAGGERING BEAUTY, DRAMA, AND POWER, Southern Utah seems like a place of myth.

Zion National Park contains stunning contrasts, with towering rock walls deeply incised by steep canyons containing a verdant oasis of cottonwood trees and wildflowers. Bryce Canyon National Park is famed for its red-and-pink hoodoos, delicate fingers of stone rising from a steep mountainside. At sunrise, the light is magical, the air crisp, and the trails nearly empty.

There are countless ways to explore the parks. Trek through narrow canyons, take in sweeping vistas on a scenic drive, or explore hoodoos up close on horseback. Whatever you choose, once you've caught a glimpse of the region's magnificence, it's likely you'll want to start planning your return trip.

Riverside Walk in Zion Canyon

BEST DAY IN
ZION & BRYCE

Morning

 Get an early start for your half day in Zion. Stop at the Zion Canyon Visitor Center to fill up your water bottles, then board the Zion Canyon shuttle (page 82).

Hop off at Zion Lodge and warm up with the easy hike to Lower Emerald Pool Trail (page 64).

3 Ride to the end of the shuttle route, the Temple of Sinawava, and follow the paved Riverside Walk along the Virgin River. Take time to admire hanging gardens, where plants grow from cracks in the cliff walls. At the end of the 1-mile (1.6-km) walk, the trail goes into the river, but water-hiking the Narrows is a seasonally accessible, full-day plunge that demands preparation. Save it for your next trip (page 71).

4 Ride the shuttle back to Zion Lodge and grab a quick lunch at the Castle Dome Café snack bar before returning to the visitor center and your car (page 79).

Afternoon

5 Leave some time to enjoy the drive to Bryce. The Zion-Mt. Carmel Highway, which leads from Zion Canyon through a series of switchbacks to a high plateau with fine outcroppings of Navajo sandstone, has plenty of roadside viewpoints and even better vistas from the 1-mile (1.6-km) round-trip Canyon Overlook Trail (page 60).

6 Once in Bryce, you'll want to get an eyeful from the Rim Trail, and then head down to commune with the hoodoos. The Queen's Garden Trail, which descends from Sunrise Point, is a favorite (page 108).

Evening

7 By this time, you'll need a real meal, so treat yourself to a sit-down dinner at the Lodge at Bryce Canyon (page 115).

8 After dinner, a stroll on the Rim Trail between Sunset and Sunrise Points will leave you with memories of glowing orange and pink spires (page 104).

9 Summer days are long, but try to stick around for sunset and join the scrum of photographers at Sunset Point. Bryce is even spectacular after dark—the lack of light pollution makes this an excellent place to view the Milky Way (page 98).

ITINERARY DETAILS

- This itinerary works best **April-October**.
- Avoid the largest crowds and intense heat by traveling **outside the July-August window**.
- Make **reservations** for **lodging and dining** up to a year in advance at Zion Lodge (888/297-2757; www.zionlodge.com) or the Lodge at Bryce Canyon (877/386-4383; www.brycecanyonforever.com); however, last-minute bookings are often available. The Lodge at Bryce Canyon is open April-October.
- Check to make sure **shuttle reservations** aren't required at Zion.
- Stuff your pack with a **picnic lunch,** lots of **water,** and **snacks.**
- **Parking** may be full, especially in summer, at Zion. Pay for parking in Springdale for easy access to the free Zion-Springdale shuttle.

Navajo Loop hoodoos

SEASONS OF ZION & BRYCE

The parks are both open year-round, although **spring** and **early fall** are the most pleasant times to visit. These are also the busiest seasons, and travelers may find that popular campgrounds and hotels are booked well in advance.

SPRING
(APR.-EARLY JUNE)

Spring rain can dampen trails, and late winter-early spring storms can play havoc with backcountry roads. Zion Canyon is pleasant in the early spring. Bryce Canyon, at elevations ranging 6,600-9,100 feet (2,012-2,774 m), can be snowy well into the spring, but it is pleasant during the summer when other areas of Southern Utah bake.

Temperatures

 Day: 54-73°F (12-23°C)
Night: 29-43°F (-2-6°C)

SUMMER
(LATE JULY-EARLY SEPT.)

Thunderstorms are fairly common in summer and bring the threat of flash flooding, especially in slot canyons. By July and August, it's quite warm in Zion, and July is the warmest month in Bryce Canyon.

Temperatures

Day: 80-100°F (27-38°C)
Night: 57-68°F (14-20°C)

EARLY FALL
(SEPT.-OCT.)

September and October are lovely times to visit Zion, with moderate

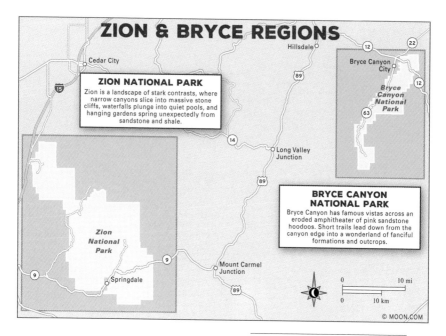

ZION & BRYCE REGIONS

Hillsdale

12

22

Cedar City

Bryce Canyon City

89

ZION NATIONAL PARK
Zion is a landscape of stark contrasts, where narrow canyons slice into massive stone cliffs, waterfalls plunge into quiet pools, and hanging gardens spring unexpectedly from sandstone and shale.

Bryce Canyon National Park

12

63

15

14

Long Valley Junction

89

BRYCE CANYON NATIONAL PARK
Bryce Canyon has famous vistas across an eroded amphitheater of pink sandstone hoodoos. Short trails lead down from the canyon edge into a wonderland of fanciful formations and outcrops.

Zion National Park

9

Mount Carmel Junction

Springdale

9

89

0   10 mi
0   10 km

© MOON.COM

a blue bellflower at the Narrows (left); a desert bighorn sheep ewe in snow-covered Zion (right)

temperatures during the day and cool nights. Be sure to pack layers, because temperatures can easily vary by 30°F during the course of the day. Late October is a good time to view fall colors in Zion Canyon. Since Bryce is at a considerably higher elevation, October visitors should pack warm clothing and not be shocked to see snow.

Temperatures

 Day: 57-78°F (14-26°C)
Night: 27-49°F (-3-9°C)

LATE FALL-WINTER (NOV.-MAR.)

A few highways in the Zion-Bryce area close for the winter, most notably the roads around Cedar Breaks National Monument. However, winter can be a great time to visit the high country around Bryce, where cross-country skiers take to the park roads. Note that winter snows can close the southern reaches of Bryce Canyon's scenic route from time to time.

Temperatures

Day: 36-48°F (2-9°C)
Night: 12-24°F (-11- -4°C)

NEED TO KNOW: ZION

- **Park website:** www.nps.gov/zion
- **Entrance fee:** $35 per vehicle
- **Main entrance:** South Entrance
- **Main visitor venter:** Zion Canyon Visitor Center
- **Hotel and park activity reservations:** www.zionlodge.com
- **Campsite reservations:** www.recreation.gov
- **Gas in the park:** None available inside the park. Gas up in Springdale, just south of the main entrance.
- **High season:** Apr.-Sept.

NEED TO KNOW: BRYCE

- **Park website:** www.nps.gov/brca
- **Entrance fee:** $35 per vehicle
- **Main entrance:** Hwy. 63 (north side of Bryce Canyon National Park)
- **Main visitor center:** Bryce Canyon Visitor Center
- **Hotel and park activity reservations:** www.brycecanyonforever.com
- **Campsite reservations:** www.recreation.gov
- **Gas in the park:** None available inside park. Gas up at Ruby's Inn, just north of the Bryce Canyon entrance.
- **High season:** May-Sept.

hiker on Angels Landing Trail in Zion (left); a view of Bryce Canyon (right)

Rainbow Point

BEST OF THE BEST
ZION & BRYCE

BEST HIKES

ZION
Emerald Pools Trails
EASY-MODERATE

Starting from Zion Lodge, hike both the **Upper and Lower Emerald Pools Trails** to small ponds, waterfalls, and verdant hanging gardens.

West Rim Trail to Angels Landing
STRENUOUS

Climb the steadily rising West Rim Trail through a series of switchbacks to Scout Lookout, gaze down on the valley, then grab hold of a trailside chain to traverse the final white-knuckle stretch to a 360-degree view at Angels Landing. (This is not a hike for kids.)

The Narrows
STRENUOUS

It's hard to say what's more of a treat—hiking through the Virgin River on a hot day or peering up at the tall sandstone walls that narrow into a slot canyon as you hike upstream.

BRYCE
Rim Trail
EASY

Stroll along the edge of Bryce Amphitheater as you take in expansive views of the park's legendary hoodoos.

Queen's Garden Trail
EASY-MODERATE

Hike down from the amphitheater rim to a little hoodoo-filled basin. This is the most intimate red-rock experience with the least effort in the park. At the bottom of the trail, a stony Queen Victoria awaits.

Emerald Pools Trails (top); West Rim Trail (bottom)

the Narrows

hikers on Queen's Garden Trail

BEST VIEWS

ZION
Court of the Patriarchs Viewpoint
For an eyeful without a hike, jump off the shuttle bus at the Court of the Patriarchs.

Angels Landing
You'll work to get here, but from Angels Landing, the views go in all directions. An early park visitor said the peak was so high, only angels could land there.

BRYCE
Sunrise Point
Though the name is cliché, the angle of the rising sun really does make Sunrise Point in Bryce special.

Inspiration Point
This cluster of three viewpoints looks over row upon row of hoodoos lining the scooped-out amphitheater below; climb a short but steep path to the highest point for real breathtaking beauty.

Yovimpa and Rainbow Points
Here at the park's highest point (9,100 ft/2,773 m), the rock cliffs making up the Grand Staircase are visible. Bryce's formations were sculpted from the Pink Cliffs; below this step of the staircase, spot the Grey and White Cliffs, with a little Vermillion Cliff layer at the bottom.

Sunrise Point (top); Court of the Patriarchs
(bottom left); Yovimpa Point (bottom right)

Angels Landing

ROAD STOPS BETWEEN ZION & BRYCE

The trip from Zion Canyon to Bryce Canyon is just over 70 miles (113 km)—a little more than an hour's drive along U.S. 89. It's just long enough that you might want some diversions along the way. Here are some worthwhile stops between Zion and Bryce. If you're starting in Bryce and heading to Zion, reverse the order.

- **Rock Shops:** There are lots of rocks in the hills—get a trunkful the easy way at the **Rock Stop** (385 W. State St., Orderville; 435/648-2747). The friendly owners also make the best coffee in this part of the state.

- **German Bakery:** Dreaming of an artisanal bakery? Head to Orderville, where **Forscher Bakery** (110 N. State St., Orderville; 435/648-3040; www.forschergermanbakery.com) makes outstanding naturally leavened breads (go for the rye) and good sandwiches.

- **Zip Line:** Soar on two zip lines (one that'll accommodate an adult and a small child) at **Mystic River Outdoor Adventures** (5000 U.S. 89; 435/648-2823; http://mysticriveradventures.com). This small family-run park north of Glendale also has a fishing pond.

- **Horseback Rides:** Even if you're not spending the night, pull off at the **Bryce Zion Campground** (5 mi/8 km north of Glendale; 855/333-7263; https://brycezioncampground.net) and saddle up for a guided trail ride. The campground makes a good base for visiting both national parks.

- **Red Canyon:** Pause and take a breath before you get to busy Bryce. Red Canyon has lots of hiking and biking trails among the red sandstone spires.

Red Canyon hiking trail

Zion-Mt. Carmel Highway

BEST SCENIC DRIVE

ZION-MT. CARMEL HIGHWAY

MILEAGE: 24.5 miles (39.4 km) one-way
DRIVING TIME: 2 hours one-way
START: Zion Canyon Visitor Center
END: Mt. Carmel Junction

From Zion Canyon, this road climbs through a series of switchbacks, passes through a crazy long tunnel (and a much shorter one), and provides access to the canyons and high plateaus east of Zion Canyon, where you'll find fewer hikers than on the canyon trails. Take the easy 1-mile (1.6-km) round-trip **Canyon Overlook Trail** to peer down at the huge **Great Arch of Zion,** a "blind" arch that's not carved all the way through. Even if you're not up for a hike, be sure to stop and admire **Checkerboard Mesa,** a huge lump of hatch-marked sandstone right at the road's edge. From the east entrance to the park, the road continues about 13 miles (20.9 km) to its junction with Highway 89. From here, head north to Bryce Canyon National Park.

Checkerboard Mesa

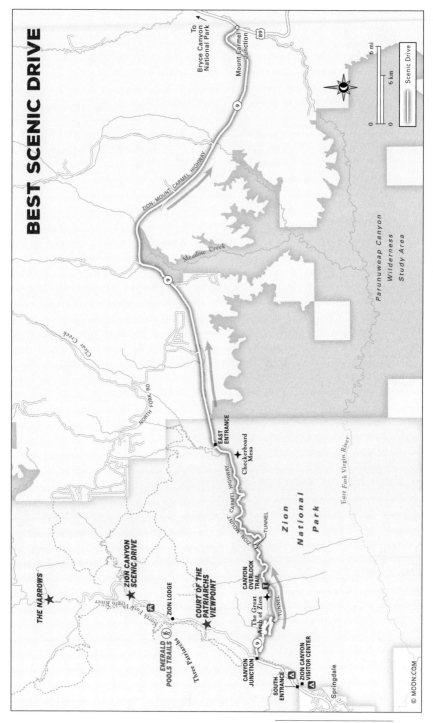

BEST SCENIC DRIVE

To Bryce Canyon National Park

Mount Carmel Junction

89

9

ZION - MOUNT CARMEL HIGHWAY

Meadow Creek

9

Clear Creek

NORTH FORK RD

Parunuweap Canyon Wilderness Study Area

EAST ENTRANCE

Checkerboard Mesa

ZION - MOUNT CARMEL HIGHWAY

East Fork Virgin River

Zion National Park

TUNNEL

THE NARROWS

ZION CANYON SCENIC DRIVE

ZION CANYON SCENIC DRIVE

North Fork Virgin River

ZION LODGE

COURT OF THE PATRIARCHS VIEWPOINT

CANYON OVERLOOK TRAIL

The Great Arch of Zion

TUNNEL

EMERALD POOLS TRAILS

Three Patriarchs

CANYON JUNCTION

9

ZION CANYON VISITOR CENTER

SOUTH ENTRANCE

Springdale

6 mi

6 km

0

0

Scenic Drive

© MOON.COM

BEST SCENIC DRIVE   35

INDIGENOUS PEOPLES OF ZION & BRYCE

It's an oddity of history that most visitors to Utah's national parks will see much more evidence of the state's ancient indigenous residents—in the form of rock art, stone pueblos, and storehouses—than they will of today's remaining Native Americans. **Ancestral Puebloans** once resided in Utah and had a settlement in present-day Zion National Park. Thousands of stone dwellings, ceremonial kivas, and towers built by the Ancestral Puebloans still stand in the state.

The Ancestral Puebloans departed from this region about 800 years ago, as did the Fremont, perhaps because of drought, warfare, or disease. (The abandonment of Ancestral Puebloan villages is a mystery still being unearthed by archaeologists.) Some of the Ancestral Puebloans moved south and joined the Pueblo people of present-day Arizona and New Mexico.

When the Mormons arrived in the 1840s, isolated bands of Native Americans lived in the river canyons. Federal reservations were granted to several of these groups.

UTE

Several bands of Utes, or Núuci, ranged over large areas of central and eastern Utah and adjacent Colorado. Originally hunter-gatherers, they acquired horses around 1800 and became skilled raiders. Customs adopted from Plains people included the use of rawhide, tepees, and the travois, a sled used to carry goods. The discovery of gold in southern Colorado and the pressures of farmers there and in Utah forced the Utes to move and renegotiate treaties many times. They now have the large Uintah and Ouray Indian Reservation in northeast Utah, the small White Mesa Indian Reservation in southeast Utah, and the Ute Mountain Indian Reservation in southwest Colorado and northwest New Mexico.

SOUTHERN PAIUTE

Six of the 19 major bands of Southern Paiutes, or Nuwuvi, lived along the Santa Clara, Beaver, and Virgin Rivers and in other parts of southwest Utah. Paiute people hunted in the area around Bryce starting in the 1200s. Historically, extended families hunted and gathered food together. Fishing and the cultivation of corn, beans, squash, and sunflowers supplemented the diet of most of the communities. Today, Utah's Paiutes have their headquarters in Cedar City and scattered small parcels of reservation land. Southern Paiutes also live in southern Nevada and northern Arizona.

NAVAJO

Calling themselves Diné, the Navajo moved into the San Juan River area around 1600. The Navajo have proved exceptionally adaptable in learning new skills from other cultures: Many Navajo crafts, clothing, and religious practices have come from Native American, Spanish, and Anglo neighbors. The Navajo were the first in the area to move away from hunting and gathering lifestyles, relying instead on the farming and shepherding techniques they had learned from the Spanish. The Navajo are one of the largest Native American groups in the country, with 16 million acres of exceptionally scenic land in southeast Utah and adjacent Arizona and New Mexico. The Navajo Nation's headquarters is at Window Rock, Arizona.

SIGHTS

The **Zion Human History Museum** contains Ancestral Puebloan artifacts. As you explore **Bryce,** keep in mind that early indigenous peoples considered some hoodoo areas to be sacred spaces, although there is no evidence to say that they worshipped the rocks themselves.

Ancient Native Americans left behind an incredible rock art legacy in Utah.

BEST GEOLOGIC FEATURES

ZION
Three Patriarchs

Three towering sandstone peaks—named by a Methodist minister for Old Testament patriarchs Abraham, Isaac, and Jacob—are best photographed when morning sunlight highlights their orange, pink, and white tones.

Great White Throne

This 2,350-foot (716-m) mountain is composed of mostly white Navajo sandstone; it's visible from many points in the canyon, but the best views are from the Big Bend shuttle stop.

the Three Patriarchs

BRYCE
"Silent City"

Inspiration Point gives a good view of this dense concentration of hoodoos and sandstone fins rising from the canyon floor. Whether the city is full of tall buildings or people standing shoulder to shoulder is up to your own imagination.

Great White Throne (left); "Silent City" (right)

SUSTAINABLE ZION & BRYCE

Bryce Canyon and Zion National Parks are actively involved with reducing the parks' carbon footprint and encouraging sustainability through a variety of initiatives. For example, both parks operate fleets of electric, battery hybrid, and alternative fuel vehicles for transportation, maintenance, enforcement and administrative purposes. In addition, both parks use specially shielded lights to minimize light pollution and to reduce the impact of artificial light on nocturnal creatures. Here's how you can help:

- Rather than driving, make use of the **shuttles** offered in both parks during high season. (In Zion, the road closes to private vehicles during high season, so use of the shuttle is compulsory.)
- Zion and Bryce also provide **recycling containers** in all guest rooms and public areas. Use them. Better yet, bring a **refillable water bottle,** as both parks have established water refill stations to reduce the use of single-use plastic water bottles.
- **Stay on marked trails,** and respect signage indicating areas that are off limits. This will help keep you safe and help preserve the trail and the environment. Creating unofficial trails or shortcuts can harm delicate plant life and expose soil to increased erosion.

Zion National Park shuttle route

Emerald Pools Trail

ZION NATIONAL PARK

ZION IS A MAGNIFICENT PARK WITH SHEER CLIFFS AND monoliths reaching high into the heavens. Energetic streams and other forces of erosion created this land of finely sculptured rock. Trickles of water, percolating through massive chunks of sandstone over the centuries, have created both dramatic canyons and an incredible variety of niche ecosystems.

The canyon's name is credited to Isaac Behunin, a Mormon pioneer who believed this spot to be a refuge from religious persecution. When Brigham Young later visited the canyon, however, he found tobacco and wine in use and declared the place "not Zion"— which some dutiful followers then began calling it.

Zion's grandeur is evident all through the year. Spring and fall provide pleasant temperatures and the best chances of seeing wildlife and wildflowers. From mid-October through early November, cottonwoods and other trees and plants blaze with color. In winter, snow-covered slopes contrast with colorful rocks. Snow may block some high-country trails and the road to Lava Point, but the rest of the park is open and accessible year-round.

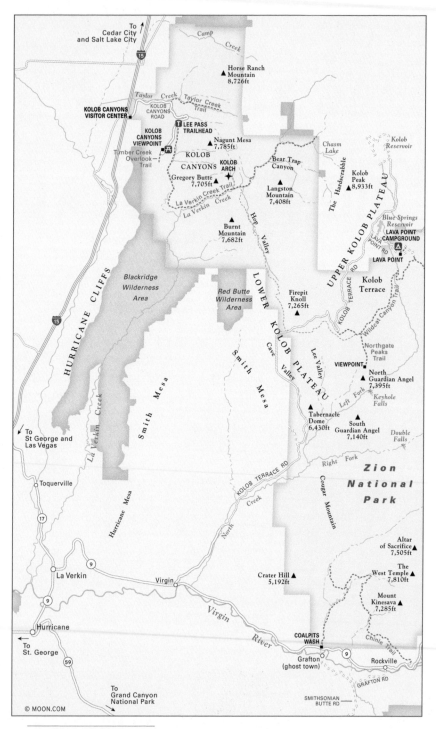

To
Cedar City
and Salt Lake City

Camp Creek

Horse Ranch
Mountain
8,726ft

Taylor Creek

Taylor Creek Trail

KOLOB
KOLOB CANYONS
VISITOR CENTER

KOLOB CANYONS ROAD

KOLOB
CANYONS
VIEWPOINT

LEE PASS
TRAILHEAD

Timber Creek
Overlook
Trail

Nagunt Mesa
7,785ft

KOLOB
CANYONS

Chasm
Lake

Kolob
Reservoir

KOLOB
ARCH

Bear Trap
Canyon

The Hardscrabble

Kolob
Peak
8,933ft

Gregory Butte
7,705ft

Langston
Mountain
7,408ft

La Verkin Creek Trail

La Verkin Creek

Hop Valley

Burnt
Mountain
7,682ft

Blue Springs
Reservoir

LAVA POINT
CAMPGROUND

LAVA POINT
RD

LAVA POINT

UPPER KOLOB PLATEAU

Kolob
Terrace

Blackridge
Wilderness
Area

Red Butte
Wilderness
Area

Firepit
Knoll
7,265ft

KOLOB TERRACE RD

Wildcat Canyon Trail

HURRICANE CLIFFS

LOWER KOLOB PLATEAU

Smith Mesa

Cave Valley

Lee Valley

Northgate
Peaks
Trail

VIEWPOINT

North
Guardian Angel
7,395ft

Left Fork

Keyhole
Falls

To
St George and
Las Vegas

Smith Mesa

Tabernacle
Dome
6,430ft

South
Guardian Angel
7,140ft

Double
Falls

La Verkin Creek

Toquerville

Hurricane Mesa

KOLOB TERRACE RD

North Creek

Right Fork

Cougar Mountain

Zion
National
Park

La Verkin

Virgin

Crater Hill
5,192ft

Altar
of Sacrifice
7,505ft

The
West Temple
7,810ft

Mount
Kinesava
7,285ft

Hurricane

To
St. George

Virgin River

COALPITS
WASH

Grafton
(ghost town)

Chinle Trail

Rockville

GRAFTON RD

To
Grand Canyon
National Park

SMITHSONIAN
BUTTE RD

© MOON.COM

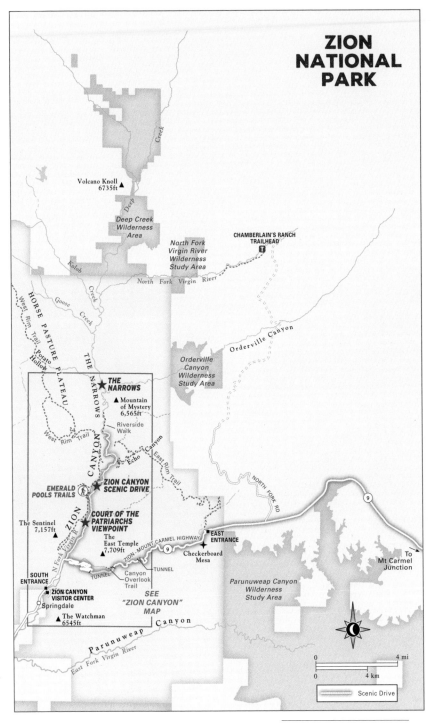

ZION
NATIONAL
PARK

Volcano Knoll
6735ft ▲

Deep Creek
Wilderness
Area

CHAMBERLAIN'S RANCH
TRAILHEAD
T

North Fork
Virgin River
Wilderness
Study Area

Deep
Creek

Kolob Creek

North Fork Virgin River

Goose Creek

Orderville Canyon

HORSE PASTURE PLATEAU

West Rim Trail

Potato Hollow

THE NARROWS

Orderville
Canyon
Wilderness
Study Area

★ THE
NARROWS

▲ Mountain
of Mystery
6,565ft

Riverside
Walk

West Rim Trail

Echo Canyon

East Rim Trail

ZION CANYON

★ ZION CANYON
SCENIC DRIVE

NORTH FORK RD

9

EMERALD
POOLS TRAILS

★ COURT OF THE
PATRIARCHS
VIEWPOINT

The Sentinel
7,157ft ▲

The
East Temple
7,709ft ▲

ZION-MOUNT CARMEL HIGHWAY

9

■ EAST
ENTRANCE

Checkerboard
Mesa

To
Mt Carmel
Junction

TUNNEL

Canyon
Overlook
Trail

TUNNEL

N Fork Virgin R

SOUTH
ENTRANCE ■

■ ZION CANYON
VISITOR CENTER

Springdale

▲ The Watchman
6545ft

SEE
"ZION CANYON"
MAP

Parunuweap Canyon
Wilderness
Study Area

Parunuweap Canyon

East Fork Virgin River

0 _____ 4 mi

0 _____ 4 km

═══ Scenic Drive

TOP 3

★ **1. COURT OF THE PATRIARCHS VIEWPOINT:** It may take a few moments to fit all three mountains into your camera's viewfinder, but the memory of the massive sandstone Patriarchs will last a lifetime (page 55).

★ **2. ZION CANYON SCENIC DRIVE:** This short drive (30 minutes one-way) winds past some of the park's most incredible scenery (page 60).

★ **3. THE NARROWS:** Step into the Virgin River to wade upstream through the high-fluted walls of spectacular canyons (page 71).

3

ZION 3 WAYS

Zion National Park has four main sections: **Zion Canyon,** a higher-elevation area **east of Zion Canyon,** the **Kolob Terrace,** and **Kolob Canyons.** The highlight for most visitors is Zion Canyon, which is approximately 2,400 feet (732 m) deep. Spring through fall, a **shuttle bus** ferries visitors along Zion Canyon Scenic Drive, which winds through the canyon floor.

HALF DAY

A half day is just enough time to ride the shuttle through Zion Canyon, admire the rock walls, and take a couple of easygoing hikes. An early start will gain you a spot in the visitor center parking lot, which gets crowded by 8am-9am. It's also possible to schedule your half-day exploration in the late afternoon and early evening; the shuttle runs until about 8pm.

1 Browse the panels in the outdoor plaza at the **Zion Canyon Visitor Center** and get in line for the shuttle. Buses come every few minutes.

2 While the morning light is still making the rocks glow, hop off the shuttle at the **Court of the Patriarchs Viewpoint** and take a very short trail to views of Abraham, Isaac, and Jacob, three Navajo sandstone peaks.

3 Ride the shuttle to the Temple of Sinawava, at the end of the line. Disembark and walk the 1-mile-long (1.6-km) **Riverside Walk** trail to its end, where longer-distance hikers may be wading into the Virgin River to continue the hike in the water.

4 Return to the shuttle and ride back to the Zion Lodge stop. Follow the paved **Lower Emerald Pool Trail** about a half mile (0.8 km) to the pool.

5 Back at **Zion Lodge,** you'll have time for a quick bite at the snack bar, or a longer sit-down meal in the lodge dining room, before returning to browse the bookstore at the visitor center and fetching your car.

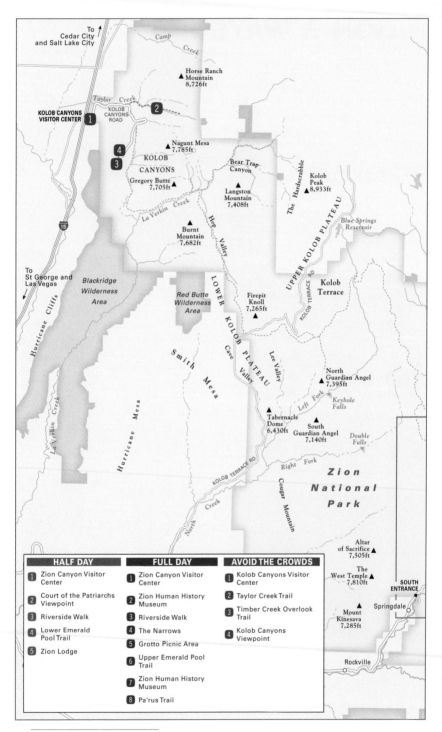

To
Cedar City
and Salt Lake City

Camp Creek

Horse Ranch
Mountain
8,726ft

Taylor Creek

**KOLOB CANYONS
VISITOR CENTER** 1

KOLOB
CANYONS
ROAD

2

4

3

Nagunt Mesa
7,785ft

KOLOB

CANYONS

Gregory Butte
7,705ft

Bear Trap
Canyon

Langston
Mountain
7,408ft

The Hardscrabble

Kolob
Peak
8,933ft

La Verkin Creek

Hop Valley

Burnt
Mountain
7,682ft

UPPER KOLOB PLATEAU

Blue Springs
Reservoir

15

To
St George and
Las Vegas

Blackridge
Wilderness
Area

Red Butte
Wilderness
Area

LOWER KOLOB PLATEAU

Firepit
Knoll
7,265ft

KOLOB TERRACE RD

**Kolob
Terrace**

Hurricane Cliffs

Smith Mesa

Cave Valley

Lee Valley

Left Fork

North
Guardian Angel
7,395ft

Keyhole
Falls

Hurricane Mesa

Tabernacle
Dome
6,430ft

South
Guardian Angel
7,140ft

Double
Falls

La Verkin Creek

KOLOB TERRACE RD

Right Fork

Zion

North Creek

Cougar Mountain

National

Park

Altar
of Sacrifice ▲
7,505ft

The
West Temple ▲
7,810ft

**SOUTH
ENTRANCE**

Springdale

Mount
Kinesava
7,285ft

Rockville

HALF DAY	FULL DAY	AVOID THE CROWDS
1 Zion Canyon Visitor Center	1 Zion Canyon Visitor Center	1 Kolob Canyons Visitor Center
2 Court of the Patriarchs Viewpoint	2 Zion Human History Museum	2 Taylor Creek Trail
3 Riverside Walk	3 Riverside Walk	3 Timber Creek Overlook Trail
4 Lower Emerald Pool Trail	4 The Narrows	4 Kolob Canyons Viewpoint
5 Zion Lodge	5 Grotto Picnic Area	
	6 Upper Emerald Pool Trail	
	7 Zion Human History Museum	
	8 Pa'rus Trail	

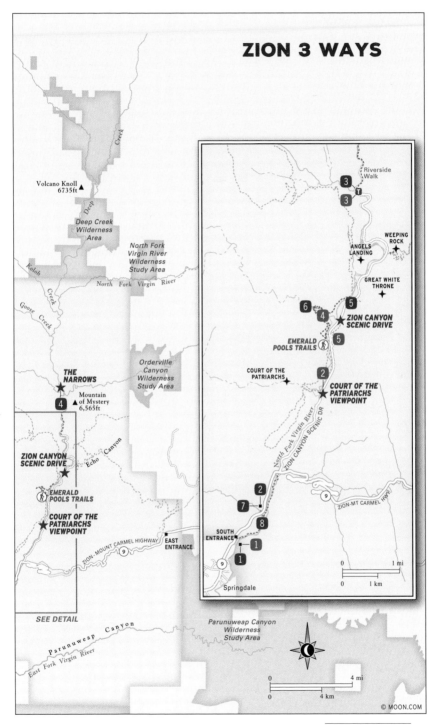

ZION 3 WAYS

FULL DAY

Your best full day in Zion includes hiking partway up the Narrows, the narrowest part of Zion Canyon. You'll actually be hiking in the river, and depending on the time of year, the water will be ankle- to waist-deep. A hiking pole or sturdy stick and shoes with grippy soles help with footing. Note that the Narrows is off limits during periods of high water flow, usually the early spring.

1 Start your day in Zion Canyon before sunrise, parking at the **Zion Canyon Visitor Center.**

2 Walk the paved Pa'rus Trail to the **Zion Human History Museum.** It won't be open yet, but its back patio is one of the park's best places to watch the sun's first rays strike the West Temple, the Towers of the Virgin, and the red-stained Altar of Sacrifice.

3 Catch the shuttle from the museum or the visitor center (or plan ahead and rent an e-bike in Springdale), ride it to the Temple of Sinawava, and walk the 1-mile-long (1.6-km) **Riverside Walk** to the start of the Narrows.

4 At the start of **the Narrows,** wade into the river and walk upstream into a steep-walled canyon. Hike up for a couple of hours and then retrace your steps (or swimming strokes).

5 After your hike, take the shuttle to the **Grotto Picnic Area** for lunch. (If you don't have lunch with you, walk the half-mile/0.8-km trail to Zion Lodge and pick something up at the snack bar.)

6 After lunch, cross the road and hike the Kayenta Trail to its junction with the **Upper Emerald Pool Trail.** Climb to the pretty green pool and hike back down the way you came.

7 Return to the **Zion Human History Museum** to watch the park movie and browse the collection.

8 Wander along the **Pa'rus Trail** as the sun sets.

AVOID THE CROWDS

Zion Canyon gets all the love—and most of the crowds. Consider heading to the **Kolob Canyons** section of the park for a quieter experience. The scenery here is different from that of Zion Canyon, with a series of parallel "finger canyons" digging into the steep rock walls.

You can start this day in **St. George** or **Cedar City;** both have plenty of hotel rooms, some good restaurants, and easy access to the Kolob Canyons. You'll be traveling along **Kolob Canyons Road,** a scenic 5-mile (8-km) stretch between the Kolob Canyons Visitor Center and the Kolob Canyons Viewpoint. Bring a bag **lunch** or some snacks with you: There's no food available in this part of the park.

1 Take exit 40 from I-15, about a 45-minute drive from the Zion Canyon Visitor Center. The **Kolob Canyons Visitor Center** is a short distance off the freeway to the east. Make a brief stop here. (At the very least, you'll need to pay the park entrance fee or show proof of payment.)

2 From the visitor center, drive 2 miles (3 km) east to the trailhead for the **Taylor Creek Trail** (5 mi/8 km round-trip), which passes through forest with historic homesteader cabins in little clearings, and ends at a cave-like alcove framed by two arches.

3 Back at the Taylor Creek trailhead, drive to the Kolob Canyons Viewpoint at the end of the 5-mile (8-km) scenic drive. The **Timber Creek Overlook Trail** starts here and travels a half mile (0.8 km) to an overlook with views of the finger canyons and the Kolob Terrace, and as far south as the north rim of the Grand Canyon.

4 Although the only camping in this area is backcountry wilderness camping, it's worth hanging around until evening. Sunset can make the Kolob's cliffs glow red, and the **Kolob Canyons Viewpoint** picnic area has some of the park's best views of the night sky.

MORE SPOTS WITH FEWER CROWDS

- Lava Point
- Canyon Overlook Trail

HIGHLIGHTS

ZION CANYON

During the busy seasons (7am-6pm final two weekends in Feb. and first weekend of March, 7am-7:30pm daily early Mar.-mid May, 6am-8:30pm daily mid-May-Sept., 7am-6:30pm daily Oct.), the 6-mile (9.7-km) Zion Canyon Scenic Drive is closed to private cars, and you must travel up and down Zion Canyon in a shuttle bus (90 minutes round-trip; free). Most visitors find the shuttle an easy and enjoyable way to visit Zion Canyon sites. The road follows the North Fork of the Virgin River upstream, passing impressive natural formations along the way, including the Three Patriarchs, Mountain of the Sun, Lady Mountain, Great White Throne, Angels Landing, and Weeping Rock. The bus stops at points of interest along the way; you can get on and off the bus as often as you want at these stops. The road ends at Temple of Sinawava and the beginning of the Riverside Walk trail. Buses are scheduled to run every 7-10 minutes.

Zion Nature Center
2pm-6pm daily Memorial Day-Labor Day

At the northern end of South Campground, the Zion Nature Center houses programs for kids, including Junior Ranger activities for ages 6-12. Although there's no shuttle stop for the Zion Nature Center, it's an easy walk along the **Pa'rus Trail** from the Zion Canyon Visitor Center or the Zion Human History Museum. Check the park newsletter for kids' programs and family hikes. Programs focus on natural history topics such as insects and bats in the park. Many Junior Ranger activities can be done on your own—pick up a booklet ($1) at the visitor center bookstore.

Zion Canyon, North Fork of the Virgin River

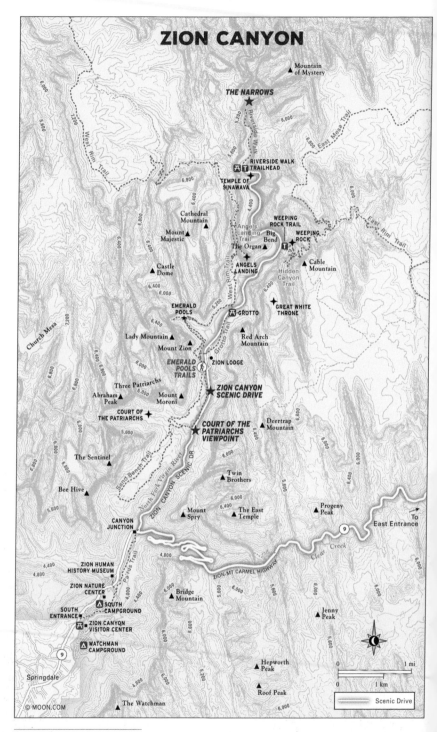

ZION CANYON

Mountain of Mystery ▲

THE NARROWS ☀

Riverside Walk

RIVERSIDE WALK TRAILHEAD

TEMPLE OF SINAWAVA

6,000

West Rim Trail

7,200

West Rim Trail

5,600

6,800

6,400

Cathedral Mountain ▲

Mount Majestic ▲

Angels Landing Trail

WEEPING ROCK TRAIL

The Organ ▲

Big Bend

WEEPING ROCK T

East Rim Trail

Castle Dome ▲

ANGELS LANDING ☀

Cable Mountain ▲

Hidden Canyon Trail

6,400

6,000

EMERALD POOLS ☀

West Rim Trail

5,200

GROTTO 🚻

GREAT WHITE THRONE ▲

Lady Mountain ▲

Mount Zion ▲

Grotto Trail

Red Arch Mountain ▲

6,400

6,000

EMERALD POOLS TRAILS

ZION LODGE

Church Mesa

7,200

Three Patriarchs ▲

Abraham Peak ▲

Mount Moroni ▲

ZION CANYON SCENIC DRIVE

COURT OF THE PATRIARCHS ☀

6,800

6,000

5,000

COURT OF THE PATRIARCHS VIEWPOINT ☀

Deertrap Mountain ▲

6,800

6,000

The Sentinel ▲

6,200

Sand Bench Trail

Twin Brothers ▲

6,400

6,000

Bee Hive ▲

5,800

5,600

5,600

6,400

North Fork Virgin River

CANYON JUNCTION

Mount Spry ▲

6,400

The East Temple ▲

Progeny Peak ▲

⑨

To East Entrance

ZION CANYON SCENIC DR

Clear Creek

4,800

6,000

ZION HUMAN HISTORY MUSEUM ■

4,400

4,800

ZION NATURE CENTER ■

Pa'rus Trail

4,000

4,400

ZION-MT CARMEL HIGHWAY

6,000

Bridge Mountain ▲

5,600

6,000

6,000

Jenny Peak ▲

SOUTH ENTRANCE ▪

SOUTH CAMPGROUND ⛺

ZION CANYON VISITOR CENTER 🚻

WATCHMAN CAMPGROUND ⛺

5,600

N

⑨

Springdale

4,800

5,200

5,600

Hepworth Peak ▲

0   1 mi

0   1 km

4,800

Roof Peak ▲

The Watchman ▲

6,000

Scenic Drive

© MOON.COM

Since Zion Canyon is nestled in between high rock walls, don't expect to actually see the sun set. But you will be able to see the rock walls glow red as the sun goes down. The **Pa'rus Trail** is a fine place to observe the changing colors.

Zion Human History Museum

Shuttle stop: Zion Human History Museum; 9am-6pm daily mid-Apr.-late May, 9am-7pm daily late May-early Sept., 9am-6pm daily early Sept.-early Oct., 10am-5pm Sat.-Sun. early Oct.-mid.-Apr.; entry included in park admission fee

The old park visitor center has been retooled as the Zion Human History Museum, covering Southern Utah's cultural history with a film introducing the park and bare-bones exhibits focusing on Native American and Mormon history. It's at the first shuttle stop after the visitor center. This is a good place to visit when you're too tired to hike any farther or if the weather forces you to seek shelter. The museum's back patio is a good place to watch the sun rise over the tall peaks of the **Towers of the Virgin,** a collection of peaks that include the **West Temple** and the **Altar of Sacrifice,** so named because of the red streaks of iron on its face.

★ Court of the Patriarchs Viewpoint

Shuttle stop: Court of the Patriarchs

A short trail from the shuttle stop leads to the viewpoint. The Patriarchs, a trio of peaks to the west, overlook Birch Creek; they are, from left to right, Abraham, Isaac, and Jacob. Mount Moroni, the reddish peak on the far right, partially blocks

Court of the Patriarchs

the view of Jacob. This is a beautiful place to relax and enjoy the view.

The Grotto
Shuttle stop: The Grotto
The Grotto is a popular place for a picnic. From here, a trail leads back to the lodge; across the road, the **Kayenta Trail** links to the **Upper Emerald Pool Trail,** and the **West Rim Trail** leads to Angels Landing and, eventually, to the Kolob Terrace section of the park.

Weeping Rock
Shuttle stop: Weeping Rock
Several hikes, including the short and easy **Weeping Rock Trail,** start at Weeping Rock; however, this shuttle stop and trailhead was closed following a huge rockfall in summer 2019. The slab of Navajo sandstone that dropped 3,000 feet (914.4 km) from the side of Cable Mountain injured several visitors (they all survived). A Utah Geological Survey report found that the area was susceptible to future large rockfalls and the park has characterized the closure as being "long term," and in 2020, park staff reported that there was no known reopening date for Weeping Rock. Check the park website for updates when planning your visit.

Weeping Rock is home to hanging gardens and many moisture-loving plants, including the striking Zion shooting star. The rock "weeps" because this is a boundary between porous Navajo sandstone and denser Kayenta shale. Water trickles down through the sandstone, and when it can't penetrate the shale, it moves laterally to the face of the cliff.

While you're at Weeping Rock, scan the cliffs for the remains of cables and rigging that were used to lower timber from the top of the rim to the canyon floor. During the early 1900s, this wood was used to build pioneer settlements in the area.

Big Bend
Shuttle stop: Big Bend
Look up: This is where you're likely to see rock climbers on the towering walls or hikers on Angels Landing. These climbers presumably are quite experienced and know what they're doing.

Temple of Sinawava
Shuttle stop: Temple of Sinawava
The last shuttle stop is at this canyon, where 2,000-foot-tall (610-m) rock walls reach up from the sides of

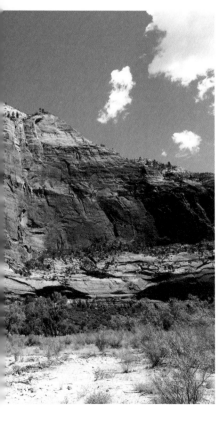

Zion Lodge (top); Big Bend (bottom left);
waterfall at Weeping Rock (bottom right)

the Virgin River. There's not enough room for the road to continue farther up the canyon, but it's spacious enough for a fine paved wheelchair-accessible walking path. Plants sprout from hanging gardens on the cliffs, and birds nest in some of the holes in the cliff walls. The Riverside Walk heads 1 mile (1.6 km) upstream to the Virgin Narrows, a place where the canyon becomes too narrow even for a sidewalk to squeeze through. You may see people hiking up the Narrows, in the river, from the end of the Riverside Walk. Don't join them unless you're properly outfitted.

KOLOB TERRACE

The Kolob Terrace section of the park is a high plateau roughly parallel to and west of Zion Canyon. From the town of Virgin (15 mi/24 km west of the south entrance station on Hwy. 9), the steep Kolob Terrace Road—now paved, though still unsuitable for trailers—runs north through ranchland and up a narrow tongue of land with drop-offs on either side, and then onto a high plateau where the land widens out. The Hurricane Cliffs rise from the gorge to the west, and

the back sides of Zion Canyon's big walls are to the east. The road passes in and out of the park and terminates at Kolob Reservoir, a popular boating and fishing destination outside the park. This section of the park is much higher than Zion Canyon, so it is a good place to explore when the canyon swelters in the summertime. It's also much less crowded than the busy canyon. Snow usually blocks the way in winter.

Lava Point

The panorama from Lava Point (elev. 7,890 ft/2,405 m) takes in the Cedar Breaks area to the north, the Pink Cliffs to the northeast, Zion Canyon Narrows and tributaries to the east, the monoliths of Zion Canyon to the southeast, and Mount Trumbull on the Arizona Strip to the south. Signs help identify features. Lava Point, which sits atop a lava flow, is a good place to cool off in summer—temperatures are about 20°F cooler than in Zion Canyon. Aspen, ponderosa pine, Gambel oak, and white fir grow here. A small primitive **campground** near the point offers sites during warmer months (free), but there is no water.

From Virgin, take the Kolob Terrace Road about 21 miles (34 km) north to the Lava Point turnoff; the viewpoint is 1.8 miles (2.9 km) farther on a well-marked but unpaved spur road. (Vehicles longer than 19 ft/6 m are prohibited on the Lava Point road.) Expect the trip from Virgin to Lava Point to take about an hour.

ponderosa pine

amazing views along the way to Lava Point

SCENIC DRIVES

★ ZION CANYON SCENIC DRIVE

DRIVING DISTANCE: 7.9 miles (12.7 km) one-way
DRIVING TIME: 30 minutes one-way
START: Zion Canyon Visitor Center
END: Temple of Sinawava

Zion Canyon Scenic Drive winds through the canyon floor along the North Fork of the Virgin River, past some of the most spectacular scenery in the park, including **the Patriarchs, Weeping Rock,** and the **Temple of Sinawava.** Also visible from several points along Zion Canyon Drive is the **Great White Throne.** Topping out at 6,744 feet (2,056 m), this bulky chunk of Navajo sandstone has become, along with the Three Patriarchs, emblematic of the park. Ride the shuttle in the evening to watch the rock change color in the light of the setting sun.

A **shuttle bus** ferries visitors along this route spring-fall, when it is for the most part closed to private cars. Hiking trails branch off to lofty viewpoints and narrow side canyons.

Water-loving adventurers can continue past the pavement's end and hike up the Virgin River at **the Narrows** in upper Zion Canyon.

ZION-MT. CARMEL HIGHWAY

DRIVING DISTANCE: 24.5 miles (39.4 km) one-way
DRIVING TIME: 2 hours one-way
START: Visitor Center
END: Mt. Carmel Junction

The east section of the park is a land of sandstone slickrock, hoodoos, and narrow canyons. You can get a good eyeful of the dramatic scenery along the Zion-Mt. Carmel Highway (Hwy. 9) between the east entrance station and Zion Canyon. Highlights on the plateau include views of the White Cliffs and Checkerboard Mesa, both near the east entrance station, and a hike on the Canyon Overlook Trail, which begins just east of the long tunnel.

- **Mile 0.0: Visitor Center**
- **Mile 1.6: Canyon Junction:** 3.5 miles (5.6 km) from the visitor

Zion-Mt. Carmel Tunnel (left); Great White Throne (right)

NAVAJO SANDSTONE

Take a look anywhere along Zion Canyon and you'll see 1,600-2,200-foot (488-671-m) cliffs of Navajo sandstone. The big walls of Zion were formed from immense sand dunes deposited during a hot dry period about 200 million years ago. Shifting winds blew the sand in one direction, then another—a careful inspection of the sandstone layer reveals the diagonal lines resulting from this **"cross-bedding."** Studies by researchers at the University of Nebraska-Lincoln conclude that the vast dunes of Southern Utah were formed when the landmass on which they sit was about 15

Navajo sandstone

degrees north of the equator, at about the same location as Honduras is today. The shift patterns in the sandstone—the slanting striations easily seen in the cliff faces—were caused in part by intense monsoon rains, which compacted and moved the dunes.

Eventually, a shallow sea washed over the dunes. Lapping waves left shells behind, and as the shells dissolved, their lime seeped down into the sand and cemented it into sandstone. After the Colorado Plateau lifted, rivers cut deeply through the sandstone layer. The formation's lower layers are stained red from iron oxides.

The east side of Zion is a particularly good place to view the warps and striations in the sandstone; get up close and personal with **Checkerboard Mesa**. But really, with the right light and a pair of binoculars, examination of Zion Canyon's big walls (the **Great White Throne** is largely white Navajo sandstone) will reveal the cross-bedding.

center. Highway 9 turns east here and begins to climb from the floor of Zion Canyon through a series of six switchbacks to a high plateau. Pullouts allow the non-acrophobic a chance to take a look at the canyon below

- **Mile 5.0: Zion-Mt. Carmel Tunnel:** This 1.1-mile (1.8-km) tunnel, completed in 1930, is narrow and a little harrowing to drive, though passengers may enjoy glimpses of park

scenery through several windows cut into the tunnel wall.

- Any vehicle more than 7 feet 10 inches wide, 11 feet 4 inches high, or 40 feet (12 m) long (50 ft/15 m with a trailer) must be "escorted" through in one-way traffic; a $15 fee, good for two passages, is charged at the tunnel to do this. Although the park service persists in using the term *escort*, you're really on your own through the tunnel. Park staff will stop oncoming traffic, allowing you enough time to drive down the middle of the tunnel, but you do not follow an escort vehicle.

- Hours for large vehicles are limited (8am-6pm daily early to mid-Mar. and late Sept.-Nov., 8am-7pm daily mid-Mar.-late April and early Sept.-late Sept., 8am-8pm daily late April-early Sept. and mid-Sept.-late Sept., 8am-4:30pm daily Nov.-early Mar.). Bicycles must be carried through the long tunnel on a car or truck; it's too dangerous to ride (hitchhiking is permitted).

- A much shorter (530-ft/162-m) tunnel to the east is easy to navigate and requires no special considerations.

- **Mile 6.1: Canyon Overlook Trail:** Just past the eastern end of the tunnel, this mile-long (1.6-km) trail leads to a viewpoint into Zion Canyon.

- **Mile 10.9: Checkerboard Mesa:** Pull off to admire this hulking rock's distinctive pattern, caused by a combination of vertical fractures and horizontal bedding planes, both accentuated by weathering. Immediately to the west of the mesa, scramble on the slickrock slope on the pass between Crazy Quilt and Checkerboard Mesas.

- **Mile 11: East entrance:** This is just a pay station, with no services.

- **Mile 24.5: Mt. Carmel Junction:** From here, Highway 89 heads north to Bryce Canyon National Park or south to Kanab.

KOLOB CANYONS ROAD

DRIVING DISTANCE: 5 miles (8 km) one-way
DRIVING TIME: 20-30 minutes one-way
START: Kolob Canyons Visitor Center
END: Mt. Carmel Junction

This scenic drive winds past the dramatic Finger Canyons of the Kolob to the Timber Creek Overlook Trail. The

Kolob Canyons Road

road is paved and has many pull-outs where you can stop to admire the scenery. The first part of the drive follows the 200-mile-long (320-km) Hurricane Fault, which forms the west edge of the Markagunt Plateau. Look for the tilted rock layers deformed by friction as the plateau rose nearly 1 mile (1.6 km). The **Taylor Creek Trail,** which begins 2 miles (3.2 km) past the visitor center, provides a close look at the canyons.

Lee Pass, 4 miles (6.4 km) beyond the visitor center, was named after John D. Lee, who was the only person ever convicted of a crime in the infamous Mountain Meadows Massacre; he's believed to have lived nearby for a short time after the 1857 incident, in which a California-bound wagon train was attacked by an alliance of Mormons and local Native Americans. About 120 people in the wagon train were killed. Only small children too young to tell the story were spared. The close-knit Mormon community tried to cover up the incident and hindered federal attempts to apprehend the killers. Only Lee, who oversaw Indian affairs in Southern Utah at the time, was ever brought to justice; he was later executed.

La Verkin Creek Trail begins at the Lee Pass trailhead and offers trips to Kolob Arch and beyond. Signs at the end of the road identify the points, buttes, mesas, and mountains. The salmon-colored Navajo sandstone cliffs glow a deep red at sunset. The **Timber Creek Overlook Trail** begins from the **picnic area** at road's end and climbs 0.5 mile (0.8 km) to the overlook (elev. 6,369 ft/1,941 m); views encompass the Pine Valley Mountains, Zion Canyon, and distant Mount Trumbull.

The Zion-Mt. Carmel Highway descends into the park (top); Checkerboard Mesa (middle); Kolob Terrace (bottom)

TOP HIKES
EMERALD POOLS TRAILS

LOWER EMERALD POOL TRAIL
Distance: 1.2 miles (1.9 km) round-trip
Duration: 1 hour round-trip
Elevation change: 69 feet (21 m)
Effort: Easy
Trailhead: Across the footbridge from Zion Lodge
Shuttle stop: Zion Lodge

This easy hike follows a paved trail to the lowest Emerald Pool. One of the highlights, at least when there's a lot of spring run-off, is the tall waterfall that feeds into the pool. At other times, and in drought years, it may be just a trickle. Although this trail is good for families and can be navigated by people using wheelchairs, it does get crowded!

UPPER EMERALD POOL TRAIL VIA KAYENTA TRAIL
Distance: 3 miles (4.8 km) round-trip
Duration: 1–3 hours round-trip
Elevation change: 350 feet (107 m)
Effort: Moderate

Trailhead: Across the footbridge from the Grotto
Shuttle stop: The Grotto Picnic Area

An oasis of pools, small waterfalls, and views of Zion Canyon make this hike a favorite. The trail to this spring-fed green pool begins at the Grotto Picnic Area, crosses a footbridge, and turns left onto the 1-mile (1.6-km) Kayenta Trail before continuing uphill to Upper Emerald Pool. This magical spot has a white-sand beach and towering cliffs rising above. Don't expect to find solitude; this trail is quite popular.

Note: Although the Emerald Pools trails are relatively easy, they do get icy and slippery in winter. More people have died from falls on the Emerald Pools trails than on the hike to Angels Landing, so do hike with attention and care.

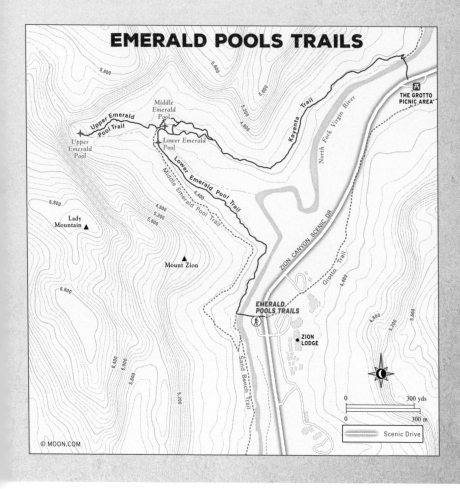

BEST HIKES

ZION CANYON

Pa'rus Trail

DISTANCE: 3.5 miles (5.6 km) round-trip
DURATION: 2 hours round-trip
ELEVATION CHANGE: 50 feet (15 m)
EFFORT: Easy
TRAILHEADS: South Campground and Canyon Junction
SHUTTLE STOPS: Zion Canyon Visitor Center and Canyon Junction

This paved, wheelchair-accessible trail runs from South Campground to the Canyon Junction shuttle-bus stop. For most of its distance, it skirts the Virgin River, and it makes for a nice early-morning or evening stroll. Listen for the trilling song of the canyon wren (easy to hear), then try to spot the small bird in the bushes (not so easy to see). The Pa'rus Trail is the only trail in the park open to bicycles and pets.

West Rim Trail to Angels Landing

DISTANCE: 5.4 miles (8.7 km) round-trip

Bikes and pedestrians (including dogs) are allowed on the paved Pa'rus Trail.

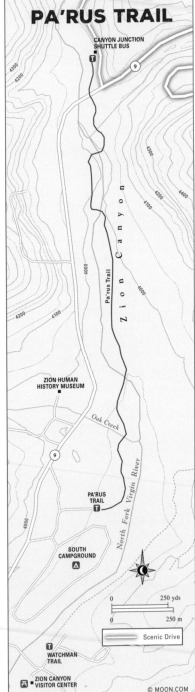

DURATION: 4 hours round-trip
ELEVATION CHANGE: 1,488 feet
(454 m)
EFFORT: Strenuous
TRAILHEAD: Across the road from
Grotto Picnic Area
SHUTTLE STOP: The Grotto

This strenuous trail leads to some of the best views of Zion Canyon. Start from Grotto Picnic Area (elev. 4,300 ft/1,311 m) and cross the footbridge, then turn right along the river. The trail, which was blasted out of the cliff side by Civilian Conservation Corps workers during the 1930s, climbs the slopes and enters the cool and shady depths of Refrigerator Canyon. Walter's Wiggles, a series of 21 closely spaced switchbacks, wind up to Scout Lookout and a trail junction—it's 4 miles (6.4 km) round-trip and a 1,050-foot (320-m) elevation gain if you decide to turn around here. Scout Lookout has fine views of Zion Canyon. From the lookout, it's a daunting 0.5 mile (0.8 km) to the summit of Angels Landing.

Angels Landing rises as a sheer-walled monolith 1,500 feet (457 m) above the North Fork of the Virgin River. Although the trail to the summit is rough and very narrow, chains provide security in the more exposed places. Hike this final approach to Angels Landing with great caution and only in good weather; don't go if the trail is covered with snow or ice or if thunderstorms threaten. Children must be closely supervised, and people who are afraid of heights should skip this trail. Once on top, the panorama makes all the effort worthwhile. Not surprisingly, it's most pleasant to do this steep hike during the cooler morning hours. Start extra early to avoid crowds, which can make the final stretch all the more frightening.

Weeping Rock Trail
DISTANCE: 0.5 mile (0.8 km)
round-trip
DURATION: 30 minutes round-trip
ELEVATION CHANGE: 100 feet
(30 m)
EFFORT: Easy
TRAILHEAD: Weeping
Rock parking area
SHUTTLE STOP: Weeping Rock

Angels Landing

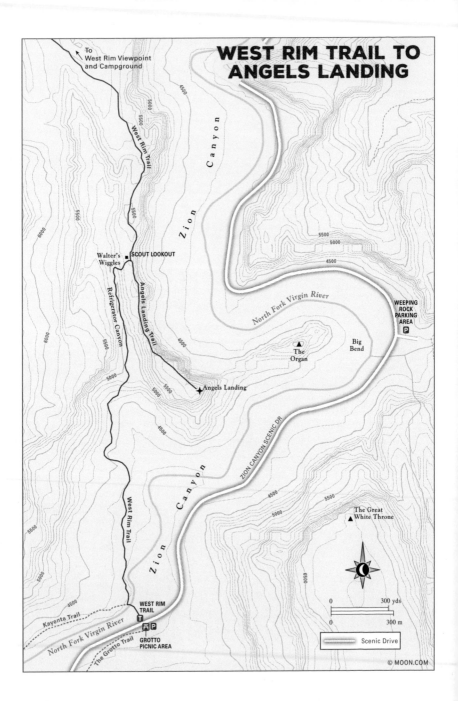

WEST RIM TRAIL TO ANGELS LANDING

To West Rim Viewpoint and Campground

West Rim Trail

Zion Canyon

Walter's Wiggles

SCOUT LOOKOUT

Refrigerator Canyon

Angels Landing Trail

North Fork Virgin River

The Organ

Angels Landing

Big Bend

WEEPING ROCK PARKING AREA

West Rim Trail

Zion Canyon

ZION CANYON SCENIC DR

The Great White Throne

0   300 yds
0   300 m

Scenic Drive

WEST RIM TRAIL

Kayenta Trail

North Fork Virgin River

The Grotto Trail

GROTTO PICNIC AREA

© MOON.COM

Weeping Rock waterfall

This easy trail winds past lush vegetation and wildflowers to a series of cliff-side springs above an overhang. Thousands of water droplets glisten in the afternoon sun. The springs emerge where water seeping through more than 2,000 feet (610 m) of Navajo sandstone meets a layer of impervious shale. Signs along the way identify some of the trees and plants.

Note: This was the site of a major rockfall in 2019 that forced the long-term closure of the trail. Check its status before planning to hike here.

Hidden Canyon Trail

DISTANCE: 3 miles (4.8 km) round-trip
DURATION: 2.5-3 hours round-trip
ELEVATION CHANGE: 850 feet (259 m)
EFFORT: Strenuous
TRAILHEAD: Weeping Rock parking area
SHUTTLE STOP: Weeping Rock

See if you can spot the entrance to Hidden Canyon from below. Inside the narrow canyon are small sandstone caves, a little natural arch, and diverse plant life. The high walls, rarely more than 65 feet (20 m) apart, block sunlight except for a short time at midday. From the trailhead at the Weeping Rock parking area, follow the East Rim Trail 0.8 mile (1.3 km) up the cliff face, then turn right and go 0.7 mile (1.1 km) on the Hidden Canyon Trail to the canyon entrance. Footing can be a bit difficult in places, but chains provide handholds on the exposed sections. Steps chopped into the rock just inside Hidden Canyon help bypass some deep pools. After heavy rains and spring runoff, the creek forms a small waterfall at the canyon entrance. The canyon itself

hikers on Hidden Canyon Trail (top); Hidden Canyon Trail (middle); columbine on the Riverside Walk (bottom)

is about 1 mile (1.6 km) long and mostly easy walking, although the trail fades away. Look for the arch on the right about 0.5 mile (0.8 km) up the canyon.

Note: The Weeping Rock trailhead was the site of a major rockfall in 2019 that forced the long-term closure of this trail. Check its status before planning to hike here.

Riverside Walk
DISTANCE: 2.2 miles (3.5 km) round-trip
DURATION: 1.5-2 hours round-trip
ELEVATION CHANGE: 57 feet (17 m)
EFFORT: Easy
TRAILHEAD: Temple of Sinawava parking area
SHUTTLE STOP: Temple of Sinawava

This is one of the most popular hikes in the park, and except for the Pa'rus Trail, it's the easiest. The nearly level paved trail begins at the end of Zion Canyon Scenic Drive and heads upstream along the Virgin River to the Narrows. Allow about two hours to fully take in the scenery—it's a good place to get a close-up view of Zion's lovely hanging gardens. Countless springs and seeps on the canyon walls support luxuriant plant growth and swamps. Most of the springs occur at the boundary between the porous Navajo sandstone and the less permeable Kayenta Formation below. The water and vegetation attract abundant wildlife; keep an eye out for birds and animals and their tracks. Late morning is the best time for photography. In autumn, cottonwoods and maples display bright splashes of color. At trail's end, the canyon is wide enough only for the river. Hikers continuing upstream on the Narrows hike must wade and sometimes even swim.

The Narrows hike, which plunges into the Virgin River, is very popular.

★ The Narrows
DISTANCE: 9.4 miles (15.1 km) round-trip
DURATION: 8 hours round-trip
ELEVATION CHANGE: 200 feet (61 m)
EFFORT: Strenuous
TRAILHEADS: End of Riverside Walk or Chamberlain's Ranch
SHUTTLE STOP: Temple of Sinawava

Upper Zion Canyon is probably the most famous backcountry area in the park, yet it's also one of the most strenuous. There's no trail, and you'll be wading in the river much of the time, which can be knee- to chest-deep. In places, the high fluted walls of the upper North Fork of the Virgin River are only 20 feet (6 m) apart, and very little sunlight penetrates the depths. Mysterious side canyons beckon.

Hikers should be well prepared and in good condition—river hiking is more tiring than hiking over dry land. The major hazards are flash floods and hypothermia; even in the summer, expect water temperatures of about 68°F/20°C (winter temps run around 38°F/3°C). Finding the right time to go through can

the Narrows

be tricky: Spring runoff is usually too high, summer thunderstorms bring hazardous flash floods or toxic cyanobacteria, and winter is too cold, unless you hike in a dry suit. That leaves just early summer (mid-June-mid-July) and early autumn (mid-Sept.-mid-Oct.) as the best bets.

Don't be tempted to wear river sandals or sneakers up the Narrows; it's easy to twist an ankle on the slippery rocks. If you have a pair of hiking boots that you don't mind drenching, they'll work, but an even better solution is available from the **Zion Adventures** (36 Lion Blvd., Springdale; 435/772-1001; www. zionadventures.com) and other Springdale outfitters. They rent specially designed river-hiking boots, along with neoprene socks, walking sticks, and, in cool weather, dry suits. Boots, socks, and sticks rent for $27; with a dry suit the package costs $57. They also provide valuable information about hiking the Narrows and lead tours of the section below Orderville Canyon (about $189 pp, depending on group size and the season). **Zion Outfitter** (7 Zion Park Blvd., Springdale; 435/772-5090; www.zionoutfitter.com), located just outside the park entrance, and **Zion Guru** (795 Zion Park Blvd., Springdale; 435/632-0432; www.zionguru. com) provide similar services at comparable prices.

Talk with rangers at the Zion Canyon Visitor Center before starting a trip; they also have a handout with useful information on planning a Narrows hike. No permit is needed if you're just going up as far as Big Springs, although you must first check conditions and the weather forecast with rangers.

A good half-day trip begins at the end of the Riverside Walk and follows the Narrows 1.5 miles (2.4 km) (about 2 hours) upstream to Orderville Canyon, then back the same way. Orderville Canyon makes a good destination itself; you can hike quite a ways up from Zion Canyon. All non-permitted day hikers must turn around at Big Springs.

EAST OF ZION CANYON
Canyon Overlook Trail
DISTANCE: 1 mile (1.6 km) round-trip
DURATION: 1 hour round-trip
ELEVATION CHANGE: 163 feet (50 m)
EFFORT: Easy
TRAILHEAD: Parking area just east of the long (westernmost) tunnel on the Zion-Mt. Carmel Highway

This fun hike starts on the road east of Zion Canyon and features great views from the heights without the stiff climbs found on most other Zion trails. The trail winds in and out along the ledges of Pine Creek Canyon, which opens into a great valley. Panoramas at trail's end take in lower Zion Canyon in the distance. A sign at the viewpoint identifies Bridge Mountain, Streaked Wall, East Temple, and other features. The **Great Arch of Zion**—termed a "blind arch" because it's open only on one side—is below; the arch is 580 feet (177 m) high, 720 feet (219 m) long, and 90 feet (27 m) deep. On a busy day, parking at and exiting from the parking area can be more challenging than the hike itself.

KOLOB CANYONS
Taylor Creek Trail
DISTANCE: 5 miles (8 km) round-trip
DURATION: 4 hours round-trip
ELEVATION CHANGE: 450 feet (137 m)

Canyon Overlook Trail

homesteader cabin on the Taylor
Creek Trail

EFFORT: Easy-moderate
TRAILHEAD: 2 miles (3.2 km) east of
Kolob Canyons Visitor Center, left side
of the road

This excellent day hike from Kolob
Canyons Road heads upstream into
the canyon of the Middle Fork of
Taylor Creek. Pass a pair of **homesteader cabins** built in the 1930s
(before the area was part of the park),
and arrive at Double Arch Alcove 2.7
miles (4.3 km) from the trailhead; a

dry fall 350 yards farther blocks the
way (water flows over it during spring
runoff and after rains). A giant rockfall occurred here in 1990. From this
trail you can also explore the North
Fork of Taylor Creek. A separate trail
along the South Fork of Taylor Creek
leaves the road at a bend 3.1 miles (5
km) from the visitor center, then goes
1.2 miles (1.9 km) upstream beneath
steep canyon walls.

Timber Creek Overlook Trail

DISTANCE: 1 mile (1.6 km) round-trip
DURATION: 30 minutes round-trip
ELEVATION CHANGE: 100 feet
(30 m)
EFFORT: Easy-moderate
TRAILHEAD: At the end of
Kolob Canyons Road, 5 miles
(8 km) from the visitor center

It's a short but relatively steep jaunt
from the parking lot at the road's end
to the Timber Creek Overlook. Along
the way, you'll have good views of
the Kolob's Finger Canyons, and on a
clear day, the North Rim of the Grand
Canyon is visible from the overlook.

Timber Creek Overlook Trail

ROCK CLIMBING IN ZION

Rock climbers come to scale the high Navajo sandstone cliffs; after Yosemite, Zion is the nation's most popular big-wall climbing area. However, Zion's sandstone is far more fragile than Yosemite's granite, and it tends to crumble and flake, especially when wet. Beginners should avoid these walls—experience with crack climbing is a must.

To catch a glimpse of these impressive athletes, be sure to look up when you reach **Big Bend** in Zion Canyon.

rock climbing in Zion

BACKPACKING

Although Zion Canyon is known for its day hikes, other areas of the park have long trails that lend themselves to overnight hikes. From the Kolob Terrace Road's Lee Pass trailhead, the **La Verkin Creek Trail to Kolob Arch** is about 6.5 miles (10.5 km), with several backcountry campsites along the way. The popular 16.2-mile (26.1-km) **West Rim Trail** starts from Lava Point, on the Kolob Terrace Road and descends to the West Rim trailhead, across from the Grotto in Zion Canyon.

PERMITS

When planning a trip, check the park's website to learn about trails and backcountry campsites and reserve a permit (see https://zion-permits.nps.gov; $5 reservation fee, $15-25 permit depending on group size). The day before your trip, convert your reservation into a permit online by contacting **zion_park_information@nps.gov.**

BIKING

One of the fringe benefits of the Zion Canyon shuttle bus is the great bicycling that's resulted from the lack of automobile traffic. It used to be way too scary to bike along the narrow, traffic-choked **Zion Canyon Scenic Drive,** but now it's a joy. When the shuttle buses get crowded (and they do), biking is a great way to get to sights up the canyon.

On the stretch of road where cars are permitted—between the Zion Canyon Visitor Center and Canyon Junction (where the Zion-Mt. Carmel Highway meets Zion Canyon Scenic Drive)—the 2-mile (3.2-km) paved

ZION NATIONAL PARK FOOD OPTIONS

NAME	LOCATION	TYPE
Red Rock Grill	Zion Lodge	sit-down restaurant
Castle Dome Café	Zion Lodge	snack bar

Pa'rus Trail is open to cyclists as well as pedestrians and makes for easy, stress-free pedaling. Bicycles are allowed on the park road, but they must pull over to allow shuttle buses to pass.

If you decide you've had enough cycling, every shuttle bus has a rack that can hold two bicycles. Bike parking is plentiful at the visitor center, Zion Lodge, and most trailheads.

Outside the Zion Canyon area, **Kolob Terrace Road** is a good place to stretch your legs; it's 22 miles (35 km) to Kolob Reservoir.

There's no place to mountain bike off-road within the park.

RENTALS

Three-speed cruiser bikes are available in Springdale at **Zion Outfitter** (7 Zion Park Blvd.; 435/772-5090; http://zionoutfitter.com; 7am-9pm daily). **Zion Adventures** (36 Lion Blvd., Springdale; 435/772-1001; www.zionadventures.com; 8am-8pm daily Mar.-Oct., 8am-7pm daily Nov., 9am-7pm daily Dec.-Feb.) rents road bikes ($35 per day) and e-bikes ($60 per day), both of which are good for park roads. **Zion Cycles** (868 Zion Park Blvd., Springdale; 435/772-0400; www.zioncycles.com; 9am-6pm daily), tucked behind Zion Pizza Noodle, has similar rentals.

American dipper along the Virgin River (top); mule deer in Zion Canyon

FOOD	PRICE	HOURS
Southwestern	moderate	6:30am-10:30am, 11:30am-3pm, and 5pm-10pm daily
fast food	budget	breakfast, lunch, and dinner daily spring-fall

HORSEBACK RIDING

Trail rides on horses and mules leave from the **corral near Zion Lodge** (435/679-8665; www.canyonrides.com; Mar.-Oct.) and head down the Virgin River. A one-hour trip ($45) goes to the Court of the Patriarchs, and a half-day ride ($90) follows the Sand Bench Trail. Riders must be at least age 7 for the short ride and age 10 for the half-day ride, and riders can weigh no more than 220 pounds.

FOOD AND LODGING

Within the park, Zion Lodge is the only place to get food or a room for the night. Look to Springdale or the east entrance of the park for more options.

ZION LODGE
**Shuttle stop: Zion Lodge;
435/772-7700 or 888/297-2757;
www.zionlodge.com**
The rustic Zion Lodge is in the heart of Zion Canyon, 3 miles (4.8 km) up Zion Canyon Scenic Drive. Zion Lodge provides the only accommodations and food options within the park. It's open year-round; reservations for guest rooms can be made up to 13 months in advance. During high season, all rooms are booked months in advance. Accommodations in motel rooms near the main lodge or cute cabins (gas fireplaces but no TV) run around $200; lodge rooms are $229-284.

The **Red Rock Grill** (435/772-7760; dinner reservations required, 6:30am-10:30am, 11:30am-3pm, and 5pm-10pm daily; dinner entrées $12-30), the lodge restaurant, offers a Southwestern and Mexican-influenced menu for breakfast, lunch, and dinner daily. A snack bar, the **Castle Dome Café** (breakfast, lunch, and dinner daily spring-fall) serves fast food; a cart on the patio sells beer.

The lodge also has public restrooms, evening programs, a gift shop, and Wi-Fi in the lobby.

BEST PICNIC SPOTS
The Grotto
Shuttle stop: The Grotto
This shady picnic area is Zion's best, with fire grates, lots of picnic tables, water, and restrooms. From here, the half-mile (0.8-km) Grotto Trail goes to Zion Lodge (where you can grab some food from the snack bar). The

ZION NATIONAL PARK CAMPGROUNDS

NAME	LOCATION	SEASON
Watchman Campground	Zion Canyon	year-round
South Campground	Zion Canyon	Mar.-Oct.
Lava Point Campground	Kolob Terrace Road	May-Sept.

Grotto itself is just a pretty clearing, but two of the park's most popular trails (leading to Upper Emerald Pool and Angels Landing) start just across the road.

Riverside Walk
Shuttle stop: Temple of Sinawava
Although it's not a formal picnic area, benches along the path offer an opportunity to watch birds nesting or feeding in the sandstone cliff. There's also wildlife-viewing (mostly deer) in the Virgin River. Use the restroom and fill your water bottle at the shuttle stop.

Visitor Center Parking Area
Shuttle stop: Visitor Center
It's convenient! Although it's close to the busy parking area, it's also close to restrooms, water, and the shuttle stop at the Visitor Center. If you need to pick up a lunch, take the short walk into Springdale and you'll find a good café almost immediately.

Watchman Campground

SITES AND AMENITIES	RV LIMIT	PRICE	RESERVATIONS
197 sites, 128 with electrical hookups ($30)	61 (no generators permitted)	$20	yes
128 sites	120 permit RVs, no hookups	$20	yes
6 sites	Vehicles longer than 19 feet (5.7 m) prohibited	free	no

Kolob Canyons Viewpoint

The views from this small, fairly primitive picnic area can stretch to the North Rim of the Grand Canyon, and this section of the park is less crowded than Zion Canyon. Hike the 1-mile (1.6-km) round-trip Timber Creek Overlook Trail for even more views. Be sure to fill your water bottle at the Kolob Canyons Visitor Center (and don't expect flush toilets at the viewpoint).

This viewpoint in the Kolob Canyons section of the park is not served by shuttle. From the Kolob Canyons Visitor Center, drive 5 miles (8 km) to the end of the Kolob Canyons Road.

CAMPING

Campgrounds in the park often fill up during Easter and other major holidays. During summer, they're often full by early afternoon, so it's best to arrive early in the day. The South and Watchman Campgrounds, both just inside the south entrance, have sites with water but no showers.

Up the Kolob Terrace Road are six first-come, first-served sites at Lava Point Campground.

Kolob Canyons entrance sign (top); bighorn sheep ram on a winter day in Zion

INFORMATION AND SERVICES

Entrance Stations

$35 per vehicle, $30 motorcyclists, $20 pedestrians or bicyclists, admission good for 7 days and unlimited shuttle use

East Entrance Station

Zion-Mt. Carmel Highway (Hwy. 9)
From the east, you come in on the Zion-Mt. Carmel Highway (Hwy. 9) and pass through a long tunnel before popping into Zion Canyon a couple of miles north of the visitor center.

South Entrance Station

Hwy. 9, Springdale
From Springdale, you enter the south end of Zion Canyon, near the visitor center and the Zion Canyon shuttle buses.

Kolob Terrace Road Entrance

Kolob Terrace Road
A third entrance leads to the less traveled part of the park and is accessed by the Kolob Terrace Road, which heads north from Highway 9 at the tiny town of Virgin and goes to backcountry sites.

Visitor Centers

Zion Canyon Visitor Center

435/772-3256; 8am-6pm daily mid-Apr.-late May and Sept.-early Oct., 8am-7pm daily late May-Aug., 8am-5pm daily early Oct.-mid-Apr.
The park's sprawling Zion Canyon Visitor Center, between Watchman and South Campgrounds, is a hub of activity. The plaza outside the building features good interpretive plaques with enough info to get you going on a hike. Inside, a large area is devoted to backcountry information; staff members can answer your questions about various trails, give you updates on the weather forecast, and help you arrange a shuttle to remote trailheads. The wilderness desk (435/772-0170) opens at 7am daily late April-late November, an hour earlier than the rest of the visitor centers. A Backcountry Shuttle Board allows hikers to coordinate transportation between trailheads.

The busiest part of the visitor center is the bookstore, stocked with an excellent selection of books covering natural history, human history, and regional travel. Topographic and geologic maps, posters, and postcards are also sold here.

Kolob Canyons Visitor Center

I-15; 435/772-3256; 8am-5pm daily mid-Mar.-early Oct., 8am-4:30pm daily mid-Oct.-mid-Mar.
Just off I-15 exit 90, the Kolob Canyons Visitor Center serves as the entrance station to this section of the park.

Although it is small and has just a handful of exhibits, the Kolob Canyons Visitor Center is a good place to stop for information on exploring the Kolob region. Hikers can learn about current trail conditions and obtain the permits required for overnight trips and Zion Narrows day trips.

TRANSPORTATION

Getting There

Car

Zion National Park is 86 miles (138 km) southwest of Bryce Canyon National Park. From Bryce, take Highway 12 west for 13.5 miles (21.7 km) to its junction with Highway 89. Turn south on Highway 89 and follow it 43 miles (69 km) to Mt. Carmel Junction and Highway 9. Turn right (west) here and travel 13 miles (21.7 km) to the east entrance of Zion. Expect this drive to take 1.5-2 hours.

Once in the park, the Zion-Mt. Carmel Highway (Hwy. 9) goes across a high plateau, through two tunnels (one a mile/1.6 km long), and down a series of switchbacks to Zion Canyon.

Parking

The visitor center parking lot fills up early and stays full all day long. If you get to Zion before 8am-9am or after 5pm-6pm, there may be parking spaces available in the visitor center lot. Campers and lodge guests can drive to their overnight spots and park there. Midday parkgoers who are staying in Springdale should stay parked at their lodging and catch the Zion-Springdale shuttle to the edge of the park. Springdale also has parking lots and some on-street parking (fees charged for both).

Zion-Springdale Shuttle

mid-Feb.-Thanksgiving, runs as often as every 6 minutes, starting at 6am during peak season; no pets allowed; free

During the high season, one line of the Zion Canyon shuttle bus travels between Springdale and the park entrance, stopping within a short walk of every Springdale motel and near several large visitor parking lots at the edge of town. The last shuttle of the day leaves the Temple of Sinawava at 8:15pm.

Getting Around

Car

Zion Lodge guests may obtain a pass authorizing them to drive to the lodge, but in general, private vehicles are not allowed to drive up Zion Canyon Road. It's fine to drive to the campgrounds; the road between the park entrance and the Zion-Mt. Carmel Highway junction is open to all vehicles. In the off-season (Nov.-Mar.), private vehicles are allowed on all roads.

It's about 40 miles (64 km) from **Zion Canyon** to the **Kolob Canyons Visitor Center;** expect the drive to take about 45 minutes to an hour. In the winter, the Kolob Canyons Road may occasionally be closed by snow.

The drive from Zion Canyon to **Lava Point** on the Kolob Terrace Road is fairly slow; plan to take about 1 hour 20 minutes to travel the 38 miles (61 km). The road is usually closed by snowfall from sometime in November until June.

From the **Zion Canyon Visitor Center** to the park's **east entrance** is less than 25 miles. Plan on taking at least 1 hour to make the drive; even if you don't stop for hikes, the speed limit is 25-35 mph and there are lots of viewpoints along the way.

Zion Canyon Shuttle

7am-6pm final two weekends in Feb. and first weekend of Mar., 7am-7:30pm daily early Mar.-mid May, 6am-8:30pm daily mid-May-Sept., 7am-6:30pm daily Oct.-Nov.

The road through Zion Canyon is narrow with few pullouts, so to keep the road from becoming a parking lot, a shuttle bus provides regular free service through the canyon. The bus line starts just inside the park entrance, at the visitor center, and runs the length of Zion Canyon Road, stopping at scenic overlooks, trailheads, and Zion Lodge.

Buses run frequently, but when the park is crowded, expect a wait. Note that during summer 2020, to comply with COVID-19 guidelines, advance reservations (www.recreation.gov; $1) were required to ride the Zion Canyon shuttle. If needed, this ticket protocol would be adopted in future years.

Most of the bus drivers are friendly, and a recording provides commentary on the sights they pass. Riding the bus is free; its operating costs are included in the park admission fee. Buses run as often as every seven minutes 6am-8:30pm daily, less frequently early in the morning and in the evening. No pets are allowed on the buses. In the off-season, November-March, private vehicles are allowed on all roads, and the buses are out of service.

descending the Peekaboo Loop Trail

BRYCE CANYON NATIONAL PARK

IN BRYCE CANYON, A GEOLOGIC FAIRYLAND OF ROCK SPIRES rises beneath the high cliffs of the Paunsaugunt Plateau. This intricate maze, eroded from soft limestone, now glows with warm shades of red, orange, pink, yellow, and cream. The sun's rays and cloud shadows moving across the landscape provide a continuous show of changing color.

Looking at these rock formations is like looking at puffy clouds in the sky; it's easy to find images in the shapes of the rocks. Some see the natural rock sculptures as Gothic castles, others as Egyptian temples, subterranean worlds inhabited by dragons, or vast armies of a lost empire. The Paiute tale of the Legend People relates how various animals and birds once lived in a beautiful city built for them by Coyote; when the Legend People began behaving badly toward Coyote, he transformed them all into stone.

Bryce Canyon isn't a canyon at all, but rather the largest of a series of massive amphitheaters cut into the Pink Cliffs. In Bryce Canyon National Park, you can gaze into the depths from viewpoints and trails on the plateau rim or hike down moderately steep trails and wind your way among the spires.

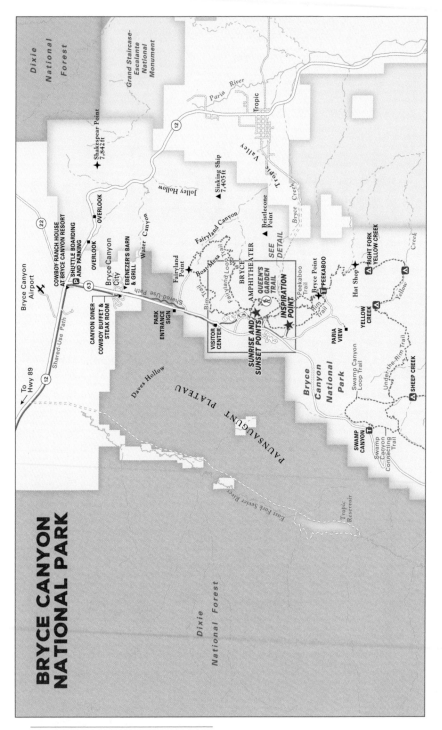

BRYCE CANYON NATIONAL PARK

Dixie National Forest

Grand Staircase-Escalante National Monument

Paria River

Tropic

Shakespear Point 7,842ft

Jolley Hollow

Sinking Ship 7,405ft

Tropic Valley

Bryce Creek

Bristlecone Point

SEE DETAIL

Bryce Canyon Airport

22

OVERLOOK

COWBOY RANCH HOUSE AT BRYCE CANYON RESORT

SHUTTLE BOARDING AND PARKING

OVERLOOK

EBENEZER'S BARN & GRILL

Bryce Canyon City

Water Canyon

Fairyland Canyon

Fairyland Point

Boat Mesa

Rim Trail

Fairyland Loop Trail

BRYCE AMPHITHEATER

QUEEN'S GARDEN TRAIL

INSPIRATION POINT

Peekaboo Trail

Bryce Point

PEEKABOO

Hat Shop

RIGHT FORK YELLOW CREEK

Creek

63

CANYON DINER

COWBOY BUFFET & STEAK ROOM

Shared-Use Path

PARK ENTRANCE SIGN

VISITOR CENTER

SUNRISE AND SUNSET POINTS

Rim Trail

PARIA VIEW

YELLOW CREEK

Yellow

12

To Hwy 89

Shared-Use Path

Daves Hollow

PAUNSAUGUNT PLATEAU

Bryce Canyon National Park

Swamp Canyon Loop Trail

Under-the-Rim Trail

SHEEP CREEK

SWAMP CANYON

Swamp Canyon Connecting Trail

East Fork Sevier River

Tropic Reservoir

Dixie National Forest

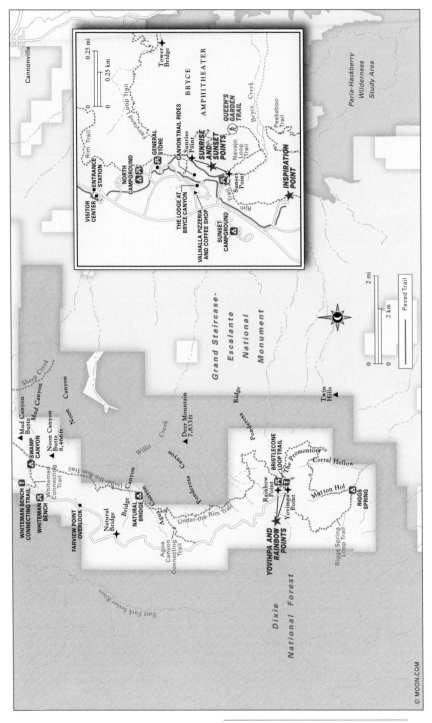

© MOON.COM

TOP 3

★ **1. SUNRISE AND SUNSET POINTS:** At the namesake hours, these overlooks are irresistible, especially if you have a camera in hand. Don't pass these up (page 98).

★ **2. INSPIRATION POINT:** From Sunset Point, walk south along the Rim Trail to see a fantastic maze of hoodoos in the "Silent City." Many rows of narrow gullies here are more than 200 feet (61 m) deep (page 98).

★ **3. YOVIMPA AND RAINBOW POINTS:** The views from this 9,115-foot-high (2,778-m) spot at the end of the scenic road are spectacular (page 103).

BRYCE CANYON 3 WAYS

HALF DAY

For a quick visit to the park, focus your time on the short, easy hikes along the Bryce Amphitheater.

1 Stop by the **visitor center** to take in the exhibits in the museum, watch the introductory film, and if the timing is right, sign up for a ranger-led talk or activity. In high season, Geology Talks and guided Rim Walks are both offered twice daily.

2 Drive (or take the shuttle in summer) to Sunset Point, then walk the **Rim Trail** from there to Sunrise Point. This portion of the Rim Trail is paved and mostly flat.

3 From Sunrise Point, take the **Queen's Garden Trail** down into the hoodoos. Follow the trail downhill among the towering rock pillars until you've seen enough, knowing that you'll need to climb back up the side of the canyon at the end.

4 Drive (or take a shuttle in summer) to **Inspiration Point** to look north over the maze of hoodoos in the "Silent City" and take in the scale of the full Bryce Amphitheater.

5 Stop for lunch or coffee at the **Lodge at Bryce Canyon,** a rustic but classy log and stone structure built in 1924.

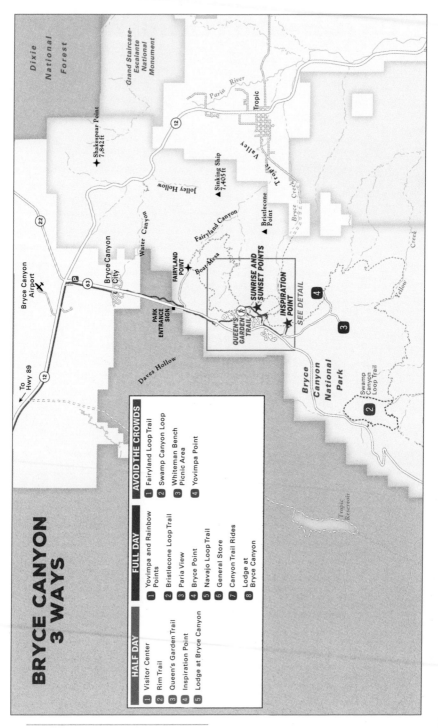

BRYCE CANYON
3 WAYS

HALF DAY
1. Visitor Center
2. Rim Trail
3. Queen's Garden Trail
4. Inspiration Point
5. Lodge at Bryce Canyon

FULL DAY
1. Yovimpa and Rainbow Points
2. Bristlecone Loop Trail
3. Paria View
4. Bryce Point
5. Navajo Loop Trail
6. General Store
7. Canyon Trail Rides
8. Lodge at Bryce Canyon

AVOID THE CROWDS
1. Fairyland Loop Trail
2. Swamp Canyon Loop
3. Whiteman Bench Picnic Area
4. Yovimpa Point

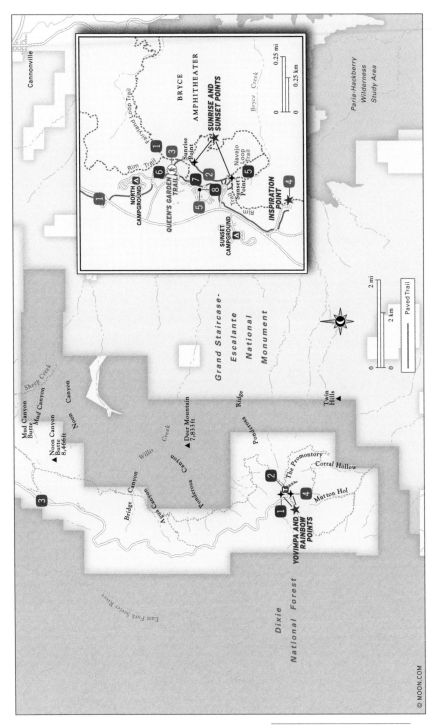

FULL DAY

Book your horseback tour with **Canyon Trail Rides** (covered here after lunch) at least seven days in advance on the outfitter's website.

1 Drive to the southern terminus of the park's scenic drive at **Yovimpa and Rainbow Points,** the highest area of the park (9,115 ft/2,778 m in elevation).

2 Walk the short **Bristlecone Loop Trail** to see small but ancient bristlecone pines.

3 Turn off the main scenic drive toward two excellent viewpoints. First up: Clifftop **Paria View** offers vistas to the south over the headwaters of Yellow Creek and Paria Canyon.

4 Your next viewpoint, **Bryce Point,** offers panoramas to the north, with the most expansive of all views over the Bryce Amphitheater.

5 Pull over at Sunset Point and put on your hiking boots. Follow the **Navajo Loop Trail** down into the canyon and amid the hoodoos until the trail intersects with the Queen's Garden Trail, which leads back up to the canyon's edge. This loop trail is 2.9 miles (4.6 km) long and will take 2-3 hours to hike.

6 Break for a quick lunch at the **General Store** picnic area nearby. The store has sandwiches and other items if you didn't bring food with you.

7 Take a two-hour horseback tour with **Canyon Trail Rides** that follows narrow trails to the base of the canyon and then back up to the rim, all accompanied by commentary on history and geology by your cowboy guide. Rides start at the horse corrals just north of the Lodge at Bryce Canyon.

8 At this altitude, evenings are chilly even in summer. Relax and enjoy dinner in front of the fireplace at the historic **Lodge at Bryce Canyon.** If you still have energy after dinner, join rangers for evening programs at the lodge or in the North Campground, or watch the night skies through telescopes as part of a ranger-led dark sky program at the visitor center.

AVOID THE CROWDS

Because the park is shaped like a long, thin string bean and is served by just one dead-end road, the farther you go south—away from the always busy Bryce Amphitheater area—the fewer crowds you'll encounter. To view and hike the amphitheater area, get up early to beat the crowds: Sunrise is a beautiful time to photograph the hoodoos.

1 Start your day at the one uncrowded trail in the busy Bryce Amphitheater area: the **Fairyland Loop Trail,** which is about 2 miles (3.2 km) north of the selfie-taking crowds at Sunrise Point. From the Fairyland Point trailhead, the entire loop back to the Rim Trail is a hefty 8 miles (12.8 km), though many people hike down far enough to see the "fairyland" of otherworldly hoodoos and then turn around and return up the same trail.

2 Next up: another hiking trail. The **Swamp Canyon Loop** drops down from the Swamp Canyon trailhead to the Under-the-Rim Trail along a pleasant seasonal stream. Connect back to the main highway along the Whiteman Connecting Trail.

3 Your hike ends at the **Whiteman Bench Picnic Area,** a pleasant, park-like layby amid ponderosa pines and white firs. Pause for lunch here.

4 At the southern terminus of the park's scenic route, **Yovimpa Point** is one of the park's highest points (9,100 ft/2,773 km) and one of the best panoramas for grasping the area's unique geologic and geographic orientation. Looking south from the point, the Grand Staircase lays out below you, like a giant multicolored layer cake, with vistas reaching as far as the northern edge of the Grand Canyon on clear days.

MORE SPOTS WITH FEWER CROWDS

- Rainbow Point
- Bristlecone Loop Trail

Unsurprisingly, the best place to be at sunset is **Sunset Point,** where the setting sun's dying rays illuminate the multihued hoodoos with deep, glowing colors. Stay in your seat after the sun has set and watch the stars and planets blink on in the darkening sky.

BRYCE CANYON SCENIC DRIVE

DRIVING DISTANCE: 18 miles (29 km) one-way
DRIVING TIME: 35 minutes one-way, without stops
START: Park entrance
END: Rainbow Point

Bryce Canyon is a long, narrow park that is served by one dead-end road. From elevations of about 8,000 feet (2,438 m) near the visitor center, this scenic drive gradually winds 1,100 feet (335 m) higher to Rainbow Point. About midway you'll notice a change in the trees from largely ponderosa pine to spruce, fir, and aspen. On a clear day, you can enjoy vistas of more than 100 miles (161 km) from many of the viewpoints. Because of

Bryce Canyon in winter

parking shortages on the drive, trailers or RVs longer than 20 feet (6 km) must be left at the visitor center or your campsite. Visitors wishing to see all of the viewpoints from Fairyland Point to Bryce Point should take a walk on the 5.5-mile (8.9-km) Rim Trail.

Note that even though the viewpoints are described here in north-to-south order, when the park is bustling, it's better to drive all the way to the southern end of the road and visit the viewpoints from south to north, thus avoiding left turns across traffic. Of course, if you're just heading to one viewpoint or trailhead, it's fine to drive directly to it.

FAIRYLAND POINT

The turnoff for Fairyland Point is just inside the park boundary, but before you get to the booth where payment is required; go north 0.8 mile (1.3 km) from the visitor center, then east 1 mile (1.6 km). Whimsical rock formations line Fairyland Canyon a short distance below. You can descend into the fairyland on the **Fairyland Loop Trail** or follow the **Rim Trail** for other panoramas.

★ SUNRISE AND SUNSET POINTS

These overlooks are off to the left about 1 mile (1.6 km) south of the visitor center, and they're connected by a 0.5-mile (0.8-km) paved section of the **Rim Trail.** Panoramas from each point take in large swathes of **Bryce Amphitheater** and beyond. The lofty Aquarius and Table Cliff Plateaus rise along the skyline to the northeast; you can see the same colorful Claron Formation in cliffs that faulting has raised about 2,000 feet (610 m) higher. A short walk down either

the **Queen's Garden Trail** or the **Navajo Loop Trail** from Sunset Point will bring you close to Bryce's **hoodoos** and provide a totally different experience from what you get atop the rim.

★ INSPIRATION POINT

It's well worth the 0.75-mile (1.2-km) walk south along the **Rim Trail** from Sunset Point to see a fantastic maze of hoodoos in the **"Silent City."** It's also accessible by car, from a spur road near the Bryce Point turnoff. Weathering along vertical joints has cut many rows of narrow gullies,

Fairyland Point (top); Sunset Point (bottom left); Inspiration Point (bottom right)

sunrise at Bryce Point

some more than 200 feet (61 m) deep. It's a short but steep 0.2-mile (0.3-km) walk up to **Upper Inspiration Point.**

BRYCE POINT

This overlook at the south end of Bryce Amphitheater has expansive views to the north and east. It's also the start for the **Rim and Peekaboo Loop Trails.** From the turnoff 2 miles (3.2 km) south of the visitor center, follow signs 2.1 miles (3.4 km) in.

PARIA VIEW

Cliffs drop precipitously into the headwaters of Yellow Creek, a tributary of the Paria River. Distant views take in the Paria River Canyon, White Cliffs (of Navajo sandstone), and Navajo Mountain. The plateau rim in the park forms a drainage divide. Precipitation falling west of the rim flows gently into the East Fork of the Sevier River and the Great Basin; precipitation landing east of the rim rushes through deep canyons in the Pink Cliffs to the Paria River and on to the Colorado River and the Grand Canyon. Take the turnoff for Bryce Point, and then keep right at the fork.

FARVIEW POINT

This sweeping panorama takes in a lot of geology. You'll see levels of the Grand Staircase that include the Aquarius and Table Cliff Plateaus to the northeast, Kaiparowits Plateau to the east, and White Cliffs to the southeast. Look beyond the White Cliffs to see a section of the Kaibab Plateau that forms the North Rim of the Grand Canyon. The overlook is on the left, 9 miles (14.5 km) south of the visitor center.

Bryce Point, one of the park's grandest vistas (top); Paria View (middle); Farview Point (bottom)

NATURAL BRIDGE

This large feature lies just off the road to the east, 1.7 miles (2.7 km) past Farview Point. The span is 54 feet (16.5 m) wide and 95 feet (29 m) high. Despite its name, this is an arch formed by weathering from rain and freezing, not by stream erosion, as with a true natural bridge. Once the opening reached ground level, runoff began to enlarge the hole and to dig a gully through it.

★ YOVIMPA AND RAINBOW POINTS

The land drops away in rugged canyons and fine views at the end of the scenic drive, 17 miles (27 km) south of the visitor center. At an elevation of 9,115 feet (2,778 m), this is the highest area of the park, and on a clear day you can see the colorful geologic layers of the **Grand Staircase,** all the way to the North Rim of the Grand Canyon. Yovimpa and Rainbow Points are only a short walk apart yet offer different vistas. The **Bristlecone**

Natural Bridge

Loop Trail is an easy 1-mile (1.6-km) loop from Rainbow Point to ancient bristlecone pines along the rim.

Yovimpa Point

BEST HIKES

RIM TRAIL

DISTANCE: 11 miles (17.7 km) round-trip
DURATION: 5-7 hours round-trip
ELEVATION CHANGE: 540 feet (165 m)
EFFORT: Easy
TRAILHEADS: Fairyland Point, Bryce Point
SHUTTLE STOPS: Fairyland Point, Bryce Point

This easy trail follows the edge of Bryce Amphitheater. Most people walk short sections of the rim in leisurely strolls or use the trail to connect with five other trails that head down beneath the rim. The 0.5-mile (0.8-km) stretch of trail near the lodge between Sunrise and Sunset Points is paved and nearly level; other parts are gently rolling.

the Rim Trail

FAIRYLAND LOOP TRAIL

DISTANCE: 8 miles (12.9 km) round-trip
DURATION: 4-5 hours round-trip
ELEVATION CHANGE: 2,300 feet (701 m)
EFFORT: Strenuous
TRAILHEADS: Fairyland Point, Sunrise Point
SHUTTLE STOPS: Fairyland Point, Sunrise Point

This trail winds in and out of colorful rock spires in the northern part of Bryce Amphitheater, a somewhat less-visited area 1 mile (1.6 km) off the main park road. Although the trail is well graded, remember the steep, unrelenting climb you'll make when you exit. You can take a loop hike of 8 miles (12.9 km) from either Fairyland Point or Sunrise Point by using

RIM TRAIL

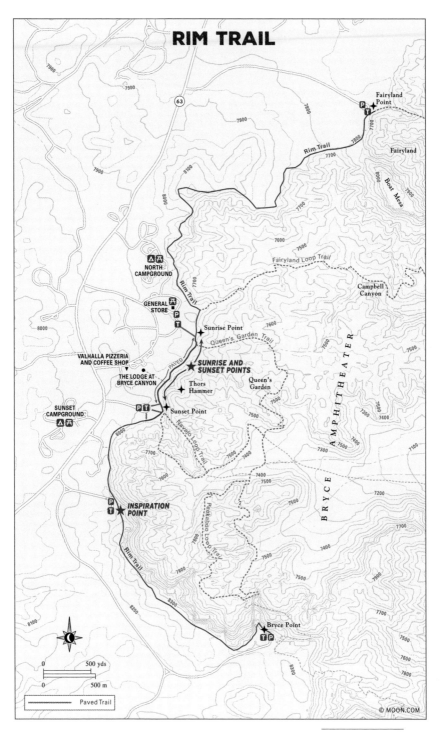

FAIRYLAND LOOP TRAIL

a section of the **Rim Trail;** a car or shuttle saves 3 hiking miles (4.8 km).

exploring the Fairyland Loop Trail

The whole loop is too long for many visitors, who enjoy short trips down and back to see this "fairyland."

NAVAJO LOOP TRAIL

DISTANCE: 1.3 miles (2.1 km) round-trip
DURATION: 1.5 hours round-trip
ELEVATION CHANGE: 520 feet (158 m)
EFFORT: Moderate
TRAILHEAD: Sunset Point
SHUTTLE STOP: Sunset Point

From Sunset Point, the trail drops 520 vertical feet (158 m) in 0.75 mile (1.2 km) through a narrow canyon. At the bottom, the loop leads into deep, dark **Wall Street**—an even narrower

Navajo Loop Trail

TOP HIKE
QUEEN'S GARDEN TRAIL

Distance: 1.8 miles (2.9 km) round-trip
Duration: 1.5 hours round-trip
Elevation change: 320 feet (98 m)
Effort: Easy-moderate
Trailhead: Sunrise Point
Shuttle Stop: Sunrise Point

A favorite of many people, this trail drops from Sunrise Point through impressive features in the middle of Bryce Amphitheater to a **hoodoo** resembling a portly Queen Victoria. This is the easiest excursion below the rim. Queen's Garden Trail also makes a good loop hike with the **Navajo Loop** and **Rim Trails;** most people who do the loop prefer to descend the steeper Navajo and climb out on Queen's Garden Trail for a 3.5-mile (5.6-km) hike. Trails also connect with the **Peekaboo Loop Trail** and go to the town of Tropic.

canyon 0.5 mile (0.8 km) long—and then returns to the rim. Of all the trails in the park, this is the most prone to rockfall, so hikers should be alert to slides or sounds of falling rocks; it's not uncommon for at least part of the trail to be closed because of the danger of falling rocks. Other destinations from the bottom of Navajo Loop Trail are **Twin Bridges, Queen's Garden Trail, Peekaboo Loop Trail,** and the town of Tropic. The 1.5-mile (2.4 km) spur trail to Tropic isn't as scenic as the other trails, but it does provide another way to enter or leave the park; ask at the visitor center or in Tropic for directions to the trailhead.

PEEKABOO LOOP TRAIL

DISTANCE: 5.5 miles (8.9 km) round-trip
DURATION: 3-4 hours round-trip
ELEVATION CHANGE: 1,500 feet (457 m)
EFFORT: Moderate-strenuous
TRAILHEAD: Bryce Point
SHUTTLE STOP: Bryce Point

overlook on the Swamp Canyon Loop

This enchanting walk is full of surprises at every turn—and there are lots of turns. The trail is in the southern part of Bryce Amphitheater, which has some of the most striking rock features. The loop segment itself is 3.5 miles (5.6 km) long, with many ups and downs and a few tunnels. The elevation change is 500-800 feet (152-244 m), depending on the trailhead you choose. The loop hooks up with the Navajo Loop and Queen's Garden Trails and can be extended by combining these loops. Peekaboo is the only trail in the park shared by horses and hikers; remember to give horseback travelers the right of way and, if possible, to step to higher ground when you allow them to pass.

SWAMP CANYON LOOP

DISTANCE: 4.3 miles (7 km) round-trip
DURATION: 2-3 hours round-trip
ELEVATION CHANGE: 800 feet (244 m)
EFFORT: Moderate
TRAILHEAD: Swamp Canyon
SHUTTLE STOP: Swamp Canyon

This loop comprises three trails: the Swamp Canyon Connecting Trail, a short stretch of the Under-the-Rim Trail, and the Sheep Creek Connecting Trail. Drop below the rim on the Swamp Canyon trail to a smaller sheltered canyon that is, by local standards, a wetland. Swamp Canyon's two tiny creeks and a spring provide enough moisture for a lush growth of grass and willows. Salamanders live here, as do a variety of birds; this is usually a good trail for birdwatching.

BRISTLECONE PINE

Somewhere on earth, a bristlecone pine tree may be among the planet's oldest living organisms. The trees here, while not the world's oldest, are up to 1,700 years old (there's a bristlecone in California that's nearly 4,800 years old). These twisted, gnarly trees are easy to spot in the area around **Rainbow Point** because they look their age.

What makes a bristlecone live so long? For one, its dense, resinous wood protects it from insects, bacteria, and fungi that kill many other trees. It grows in a harsh dry climate where there's not a lot of competition from other plants. During

bristlecone pine

droughts that would kill most other plants, the bristlecone can slow its metabolism until it's practically dormant, then spring back to life when conditions are less severe. Although the dry desert air poses its own set of challenges, it also keeps the tree from rotting.

Besides its ancient look, a bristlecone pine can be recognized by its distinctive needles—they're packed tightly, five to a bunch, with the bunches running along the length of a branch, making it look like a bottle brush.

BRISTLECONE LOOP TRAIL

DISTANCE: 1 mile (1.6 km) round-trip
DURATION: 30 minutes–
1 hour round-trip
ELEVATION CHANGE: 195 feet (59 m)
EFFORT: Easy
TRAILHEADS: Rainbow Point, Yovimpa Point
SHUTTLE STOP: Rainbow Point

This easy 1-mile (1.6-km) loop begins from either Rainbow or Yovimpa Point and goes to viewpoints and ancient bristlecone pines along the rim. These hardy trees survive fierce storms and extremes of hot and cold that no other tree can. Some of the bristlecone pines here are 1,700 years old.

BACKPACKING

Most trails in Bryce Canyon are for day hikes that explore the hoodoos in the Bryce Amphitheater, though the southern reaches of the park offer a couple of opportunities for overnight backpacking trips. All overnight camping trips require a backcountry **permit** ($5 per person per night).

The park's longest trail is the 23-mile (37-km) **Under-the-Rim Trail** that runs from Rainbow Point, at the end of the park's scenic route, to Bryce Point. It's considered a fairly arduous trail, and for most hikers will require at least two days to complete. There are five backcountry campgrounds along the trail. If you don't want to commit to the entire trail, four different connector trails lead back to the rim and the scenic route, making it possible to break this trek into shorter hikes.

Also departing from Rainbow Point, the 8.5-mile (13.7-km) **Riggs Spring Loop Trail** is a fairly strenuous hike with plenty of elevation change. With three campgrounds along the trail, it's usually considered a good overnight backpacking trip.

HORSEBACK RIDING

CANYON TRAIL RIDES
Lodge at Bryce Canyon; 435/679-8665; www.canyonrides.com; Apr.-Oct.

If you'd like to get down among the hoodoos but aren't sure you'll have the energy to hike back up to the rim, consider letting a horse help you along. Canyon Trail Rides, a park concessionaire, offers two-hour ($65) and half-day ($90) guided rides near Sunrise Point. Both rides descend to the floor of the canyon; the longer ride follows the Peekaboo Loop Trail. Riders must be at least seven years old and weigh no more than 220 pounds (99 kg); the horses and wranglers are accustomed to novices.

Sunset Campground (top); horses in Bryce Canyon National Park (bottom right); snowy trail in Bryce Canyon (bottom left)

BRYCE CANYON NATIONAL PARK FOOD OPTIONS

NAME	LOCATION	TYPE
★ Lodge at Bryce Canyon	Bryce Lodge	sit-down restaurant
Valhalla Pizzeria and Coffee Shop	Bryce Lodge	quick meals and takeout
General Store	Sunrise Point	takeout
Cowboy Buffet and Steak Room	Ruby's	sit-down restaurant
Canyon Diner	Ruby's	quick meals and takeout
Ebenezer's Barn & Grill	Ruby's	sit-down restaurant and entertainment
Cowboy Ranch House at Bryce Canyon Resort	Bryce Canyon Resort	sit-down restaurant and entertainment

RUBY'S HORSEBACK ADVENTURES
435/834-5341 or 866/782-0002; www.horserides.net; Apr.-Oct.
Ruby's Horseback Adventures offers horseback riding in and near Bryce Canyon. There's a choice of half-day ($90) and full-day ($135, including lunch) trips, as well as a 1.5-hour trip ($68). During the summer, Ruby's also sponsors a rodeo (7pm Wed.-Sat.; $14 adults; $9 ages 5-11) across from the inn.

WINTER SPORTS

Although Bryce is most popular during the summer months (Apr.-Oct. being the most popular times to visit), it is especially beautiful and otherworldly during the winter, when the rock formations are topped with snow. Because Bryce is so high (elevation ranges 8,000-9,000 ft/2,438-2,743 m), winter lasts a long time, often into April.

SNOWSHOEING AND CROSS-COUNTRY SKIING
The main park roads and most viewpoints are plowed, and the Rim Trail is an excellent, easy snowshoe or cross-country ski route. The roads to Paria View and Fairyland Point remain unplowed and are marked as **Paria Ski Trail** (a 5-mi/8-km

FOOD	PRICE	HOURS
regional American	moderate	7am-10am, noon-3pm, and 5pm-9pm daily Apr.-Oct.
pizza	moderate	6am-10pm daily mid-May-mid-Oct.
pizza and sandwiches	budget	11:30am-5pm daily Apr.-Dec.
classic American	moderate	6:30am-9:30pm daily summer, 6:30am-9pm winter
casual American	budget	6:30am-9:30pm daily May-mid-Oct., noon-7pm mid-Oct.-Apr.
cowboy-style food	moderate	7pm dinner, 8pm show daily late Apr.-mid-Oct.
casual American	moderate	7am-10pm daily

loop) and **Fairyland Ski Trail** (a 2.5-mi/4-km loop) for snowshoers and cross-country skiers. Rent cross-country ski equipment just outside the park at Ruby's Inn (26 S. Main St.; 435/834-5341 or 866/866-6616; www.rubysinn.com).

The **Bryce Canyon Snowshoe Program** (435/834-4747; 1pm daily when possible; free) offers free snowshoes and poles when you join a guided hike with a snowshoe ranger. These 1-mile (1.6-km) outings are designed for beginners and depend on snow depth and ranger availability. On full-moon nights November to March, rangers add a moonlit snowshoe hike.

Although trail closures are relatively common due to rockfall or slick conditions, winter can be a fabulous time to get into the hoodoos. Crampons or simpler traction devices (such as Yaktrax) are often far safer than snowshoes for hiking steep trails with packed snow or ice.

FOOD

LODGE AT BRYCE CANYON

435/834-8700; www.brycecanyon-forever.com; 7am-10am, noon-3pm, and 5pm-9pm daily Apr.-Oct.; $17-34

The dining room at the Lodge at Bryce Canyon is classy and atmospheric, with a large stone fireplace and white tablecloths, and offers food that's better than anything else

BRYCE CANYON NATIONAL PARK CAMPGROUNDS

NAME	LOCATION	SEASON
North Campground	Visitor Center	at least one loop open year-round
Sunset Campground	Sunset Campground	late spring-early fall

you're going to find in the area. For lunch ($10-15), the snack bar is a good bet in nice weather; the only seating is outside on the patio or in the hotel lobby.

BEST PICNIC SPOTS
Sunset Point
Shuttle stop: Sunset Point
This popular picnic area is right along the Rim Trail, with easy access to parking and restrooms. As the name suggests, this viewpoint offers great vistas as the setting sun illuminates the hoodoos, so this is a wonderful spot for your evening meal.

General Store
Shuttle stop: Sunrise Point
If you didn't bring your own picnic supplies, it's handy to know that you can buy sandwiches and other convenience foods at the General Store and then use the adjacent picnic area for al fresco dining. A restroom is also available.

picnic with a view at Rainbow Point

SITES AND AMENITIES	RV LIMIT	PRICE	RESERVATIONS
about 100 sites	14 days; no max number of RVs	$20 tents, $30 RVs	no
about 100 sites	14 days; no max number of RVs	$20 tents, $30 RVs	yes

North Campground Picnic Area
Shuttle Stop: Sunrise Point

The park's North Campground also offers a picnic area not far from the Rim Trail and in a pleasant woodsy setting. Grills are available if you want to cook over a fire, and bathrooms are a short stroll away.

Whiteman Bench Picnic Area
Shuttle Stop: Whiteman Bench

If picnicking with the crowds along the Bryce Amphitheater is not for you, Whiteman Bench Picnic Area offers relative solitude 9.5 miles (15.2 km) south of the park entrance, along the scenic road toward Rainbow Point. The picnic area is also the trailhead for the Whiteman Connection Trail to the long-distance Under-the-Rim Trail.

Rainbow Point
Shuttle Stop: Rainbow Point

At the southern terminus of the park's scenic drive, the Rainbow Point Picnic Area is 18 miles (29 km) south of the park entrance. In addition to epic views, the picnic area offers grills areas and restrooms.

CAMPING

The park's two campgrounds both have water and some pull-through spaces.

Reservations (877/444-6777; www.recreation.gov; May-Oct.) are accepted seasonally for Sunset Campground; North Campground is first come-first served. Make reservations at least two days in advance. Otherwise, try to arrive early for a space during the busy summer season, because both campgrounds usually fill by 1pm or 2pm.

Basic groceries, camping supplies, coin-operated showers, and a laundry room are available at the General Store (mid-Apr.-late Sept.), between North Campground and Sunrise Point. During the rest of the year, you can go outside the park to Ruby's Inn for these services.

LODGING

Travelers may have a hard time finding accommodations April-October in both the park and nearby areas. Advance reservations at lodges and motels are a good idea; otherwise, plan to arrive by late morning if you expect to find a room without reservations. You'll also find that there's a huge variation in room prices from day to day and from season to season. Use the prices cited below, for summer high season, only as a general guide; what you may find on the Internet or by phone on a particular evening may differ markedly.

The Lodge at Bryce Canyon is the only lodge inside the park, and you'll generally need to make reservations months in advance to get a room at this historic landmark (although it doesn't hurt to ask about last-minute vacancies). Other motels are clustered near the park entrance road, but many do not offer much for the money. The quality of lodgings is generally quite low in areas around the park; they're somewhat better in Tropic, 11 miles (17.7 km) east on Highway 12, and in Panguitch, 25 miles (40 km) to the northwest.

LODGE AT BRYCE CANYON

435/834-8700 or 877/386-4383; www.brycecanyonforever.com; Apr.-Oct.; rooms $223-271, cabins $231

Set among ponderosa pines a short walk from the rim, the Lodge at Bryce Canyon was built in 1923 by a division of the Union Pacific Railroad; a spur line once terminated at the front entrance. The lodge is the only lodging in the park itself and has lots of charm; it's listed in the National Register of Historic Places. It also has by far the best location

---

The Lodge at Bryce Canyon was built by the Union Pacific Railroad in 1923.

BRYCE CANYON FESTIVALS

Several festivals offer a chance to dig a little deeper into the park's astronomy, geology, and natural history. Although these are regular events, dates vary from year to year; check the park's website (www.nps.gov/brca) for details.

If you want to delve into Bryce's geology, plan a trip in mid-July, when the free two-day **GeoFest** offers geologist-guided hikes and bus tours as well as evening programs, exhibits, and activities for kids. Check under Things To Do on the park's website for more information. Reserve seats on the bus tour in advance by calling 435/834-5290 and pick up tickets for guided hikes at the visitor center.

Bryce has been designated a Night Sky Sanctuary, and it's a great place to stargaze. Check the park's website for the date of the June **Astronomy Festival,** when you can explore stars, the planets, and the Milky Way in one of the darkest spots in the Lower 48. During the day, there's safe solar viewing through special telescopes at the visitor center, a workshop on telescope basics, and a star lab in the lodge auditorium. Evening talks get visitors ready for stargazing through huge telescopes. Special shuttles run to the stargazing site; check at the visitor center or visit the park website for full schedules and shuttle details.

night sky in Bryce Canyon

of any Bryce-area accommodations. Options include suites in the lodge, motel-style guest rooms, and lodgepole pine cabins; all are clean and pleasant but fairly basic in terms of amenities. Reserving up to a year in advance is a good idea for the busy spring, summer, and early fall season; these are popular lodgings.

Activities at the lodge include horseback rides, park tours, evening entertainment, and ranger talks. A gift shop sells souvenirs, while food can be found at both a restaurant and a snack bar.

INFORMATION AND SERVICES

Entrance Station

$35 per vehicle, $30 motorcycles, $20 pp cyclists or pedestrians, admission good for 7 days and unlimited shuttle use

From Highway 12, Highway 63 heads 3 miles (4.8 km) south to enter the park, where it becomes the main park road, going all the way south to Rainbow Point. This is the only way to enter the park; there are no other entrance stations.

Visitor Center

435/834-4747; 8am-8pm daily May-Sept., 8am-6pm daily mid-Mar.-Apr. and Oct., 8am-4:30pm daily Nov.-mid-Mar.

From the turnoff on Highway 12, follow signs past Ruby's Inn for 4.5 miles (7.2 km) south to the park entrance; the visitor center is a short distance farther on the right. A 20-minute video, shown every half hour, introduces the park. Geologic exhibits illustrate how the land was formed and how it has changed. Historical displays cover the Paiute people, early nonnative explorers, and the first settlers; trees, flowers, and wildlife are identified. Rangers present a variety of naturalist programs, including short hikes, mid-May-early September; see the posted schedule.

TRANSPORTATION

Getting There

Car

Bryce Canyon National Park is just south of the incredibly scenic Highway 12, between Bryce Junction and Tropic. To reach the park from Bryce Junction (7 mi/11.3 km south of Panguitch at the intersection of U.S. 89 and Hwy. 12), head 14 miles (22.5 km) east on Highway 12, then south 3 miles (4.8 km) on Highway 63. From Escalante, it's about 50 miles (80.4 km) west on Highway 12 to the turnoff for Bryce; turn south onto Highway 63 for the final 3 miles (4.8 km) into the park (winter snows occasionally close this section). Both approaches have spectacular scenery.

From Zion National Park

Bryce Canyon National Park is 84 miles (135 km) from Zion. From Zion Canyon, head east via the Zion-Mt. Carmel Highway (Hwy. 9); it's 24.5 miles (39 km) to its junction with U.S. 89. Turn north and follow U.S. 89 for 42 miles (67.5 km) to Bryce Junction. Turn east onto Highway 12 and travel 14 miles (22.5 km). Turn south on Highway 63; the entrance to Bryce Canyon National Park is 3 miles (4.8 km) down the road.

Parking

Free parking is available at the visitor center or near Ruby's Inn, outside the park entrance but near shuttle bus stops.

Getting Around

Car

You can drive your own vehicle into Bryce Canyon National Park. However, if you do drive into the park, don't plan to pull a trailer all the way to Rainbow Point: Trailers aren't allowed past Sunset Campground. Trailer parking is available at the visitor center.

Although all Bryce's main viewpoints and trailheads have parking lots, they can fill up by mid-morning. Note that tour buses roll in and out throughout much of the day, especially around Sunrise and Sunset Points. Although a fair number of visitors just sneak a peek and a selfie and return to their cars, making turnover about like a crowded grocery store lot, taking the park shuttle may save you a bit of tooth gnashing.

Note that large RVs (any rig over 20 ft/6 m) are prohibited from parking in the Bryce Amphitheater (Sunrise, Sunset, Inspiration, Bryce, and Paria Viewpoints), as well as at the Lodge at Bryce Canyon and main Visitor Center lot, during shuttle hours. They also can't drive the park road beyond the turnoff to Inspiration, Bryce, and Paria Viewpoints. Plan to park at the Additional Parking Lot across from the Visitor Center, the Shuttle Station parking lot across from Ruby's Inn, or your campsite, and use the park shuttle to get around.

Bryce Canyon Shuttle

every 15-20 minutes 8am-8pm daily mid-April-mid-Oct., shorter hours early and late in season; free

During the summer, Bryce hosts an enormous number of visitors. In order to keep the one main road along the rim from turning into a parking lot, the National Park Service runs the Bryce Canyon Shuttle. Buses run during the peak summer season from the shuttle parking and boarding area at the intersection of Highways 12 and 63 to the visitor center, with stops at Ruby's Inn and Ruby's Campground. From the visitor center, the shuttle travels to the park's developed areas, including all the main amphitheater viewpoints, Sunset Campground, and the Lodge at Bryce Canyon. Passengers can take as long as they like at any viewpoint, then catch a later bus. The shuttle bus service also makes it easier for hikers, who don't need to worry about car shuttles between trailheads.

Use of the shuttle bus system is included in the cost of admission to the park, but it is not mandatory; you can still bring in your own vehicle. However, park officials note that there is generally one parking space for every four cars entering the park.

the Checkerboard Mesa

GEOLOGY

WHEN YOU VISIT ANY ONE OF UTAH'S NATIONAL PARKS, THE first things you're likely to notice are rocks. Vegetation is sparse and the soil is thin, so there's not much to hide the geology here. Particularly stunning views are found where rivers have carved deep canyons through the rock layers.

The clean, orderly stairsteps from the young rocks in Bryce Canyon to the much older Grand Canyon show off the clearly defined layers of rock. Weird crenellations, hoodoos, and arches occur as a result of the way erosion acted on the various rocks that make up this big Colorado Plateau layer cake.

CRYPTOBIOTIC SOIL

Over much of the Colorado Plateau, the soil is alive. What looks like a grayish-brown crust is actually a dense network of filament-forming blue-green algae intertwined with soil particles, lichens, moss, green algae, and microfungi. This slightly sticky, crusty mass holds the soil together, slowing erosion. Its sponge-like consistency allows it to soak up water and hold it. Plants growing in cryptobiotic soil have a great advantage over plants rooted in dry sandy soil.

Cryptobiotic soils take a long time to develop and are extremely fragile. Make every effort to avoid stepping on them—stick to trails, slickrock, or rocks instead.

HOODOOS

Hoodoos are thin spires or columns of stone that in Bryce Canyon National Park have eroded from layers of colorful sedimentary deposits. The hoodoos here stand in rows of straight alignment, giving the impression of ranks of marching soldiers, or the remnants of ancient temples. Although many visitors assume that wind shaped Bryce Canyon's hoodoos, they were, in fact, formed by water, ice, and gravity, and the way those elements and forces have interacted over the years on rocks of varying hardness.

When the Colorado Plateau uplifted, vertical breaks—called joints—formed in the plateau. Joints allowed water to flow into the rock. As water flowed through these joints, erosion widened them into rivulets, gullies, and eventually deep slot canyons. Even more powerful than water, the action of ice freezing, melting, then freezing again, as it does about 200 days a year at Bryce, causes ice wedges to form within the rock joints, eventually breaking the rock.

a hiker explores Bryce Canyon (top); hoodoos from Bryce Point (bottom left); ice, wind, and rain have carved the hoodoos in Bryce Canyon (bottom right)

hoodoos along the Queen's Garden Trail

ZION'S ROCK FORMATIONS

What Zion lacks in hoodoos, it makes up for in other distinctive rock formations:

The Patriarchs

Views of these three sandstone peaks (named Abraham, Isaac, and Jacob) are accessible via a short trail from the **Court of the Patriarchs Viewpoint** in Zion National Park (page 55).

Great White Throne

A chunk of Navajo sandstone that (along with the Patriarchs) is emblematic of Zion National Park. It's visible from various points along **Zion Canyon Scenic Drive,** and particularly lovely at sunset (page 60).

Checkerboard Mesa

This hulking rock's distinctive pattern was caused by a combination of vertical fractures and horizontal bedding planes, both accentuated by weathering. View it as you drive from Zion towards Bryce along the **Zion-Mt. Carmel Highway** (page 62).

Checkerboard Mesa's unusual façade is caused by oppositional fracturing.

Bryce Canyon is composed of layers of limestone, siltstone, dolomite, and mudstone. Each rock type erodes at a different rate, carving the strange shapes of the hoodoos. The word *hoodoo* derives from the same sources as *voodoo;* both words are sometimes used to describe folk beliefs and practices. Early Spanish explorers transferred the mystical sense of the word to the towering, vaguely humanoid rock formations that rise above Southwestern landscapes. The Spaniards believed that Native Americans worshipped these statue-like "enchanted rocks." In fact, while early indigenous people considered many hoodoo areas sacred, there is no evidence that they worshipped the stones themselves.

WHERE TO SEE HOODOOS

- Rim Trail (page 104)
- Bryce Point (page 102)
- Inspiration Point (page 98)
- Queen's Garden Trail (page 108)
- Riggs Spring Loop (page 112)
- Zion-Mt. Carmel Highway (page 60)

ARCHES

Although Zion and Bryce Canyon aren't known for their rock arches (unlike southeast Utah's Arches National Park), these parks do share the same underlying rock formations, and when these formations are exposed, arches will form. An unusual combination of geologic forces is responsible for the creation of arches. About 300 million years ago, evaporation of inland seas left behind a salt layer more than 3,000 feet (915 m) thick in the Paradox Basin of southern Utah. Sediments,

the Great Arch of Zion

Natural Bridge

including those that later became the arches, then covered the salt. Unequal pressures caused the salt to gradually flow upward in places, bending the overlying sediments as well. These upfolds, or anticlines, later collapsed when groundwater dissolved the underlying salt.

The faults and joints caused by the uplift and collapse opened the way for erosion to carve freestanding rock fins. The fins' uniform strength and hard upper surfaces have proved ideal for arch formation. Alternate freezing and thawing action and exfoliation (flaking caused by expansion when water or frost penetrates the rock) continued to peel away the softer rock until holes formed in some of the fins. Rockfalls within the holes helped enlarge the arches.

A number of terms are used to describe rock arches. Although the term "windows" often refers to openings in large walls of rock, windows and arches are really the same. Arches are also sometimes referred to as rock bridges, but geologically speaking, rock bridges have live streams running through them, while arches do not.

WHERE TO SEE ARCHES

- Canyon Overlook Trail (page 74)
- Natural Bridge (page 103)

HANGING GARDENS

Look along Zion's Virgin River canyon for clumps of ferns and mosses lit with maidenhair ferns, shooting stars, monkey flowers, columbine, orchids, and bluebells. These unexpectedly lush pockets are called "hanging gardens," gemlike islands of plant life nestled into canyon walls.

Hanging gardens take advantage of a unique microclimate

columbine plants along Riverside Walk

hanging gardens (left); columbine flower (right)

created by the meeting of two rock layers: Navajo sandstone and Kayenta shale. Water percolates down through porous sandstone and, when it hits the denser shale layer, travels laterally along the top of the harder rock and emerges at cliff's edge. These little springs support lush plant life.

Although spring and early summer are peak times for wildflower blooms, the trickles of water keep plants looking pretty good even during the summer's heat.

WHERE TO SEE HANGING GARDENS

- Emerald Pools Trails (page 64)
- Weeping Rock Trail (page 67)
- Temple of Sinawava (page 56)
- Riverside Walk (page 71)

COLORFUL ROCKS

In Utah, you'll get used to seeing a lot of colorful rock formations. The color gives you clues to the composition and geologic history of the rock. In general:

Red rocks are stained by rusty iron-rich sediments washed down from mountains, and they are a clue that erosion has occurred.

Gray or brown rocks were deposited by ancient seas.

White rocks are colored by their "glue," the limey remains of dissolved seashells that leach down and harden sandstones.

Black rocks are volcanic in origin, though not all volcanic, or igneous, rocks are black. Igneous rocks are present in the La Sal, Abajo, and Henry Mountains near Canyonlands. These mountains are "laccoliths," formed by molten magma that pushed through the sedimentary layers, leaking deeper into some layers than others and eventually forming broad dome-shaped protuberances, which were eroded into soft peaks, then carved by glaciers into the sharp peaks we see today.

A layer of lava also caps the Paunsaugunt, Markagunt, and Aquarius Plateaus, which have lifted above the main level of the Colorado Plateau. This mostly basalt layer was laid down about 37 million years ago, before the Colorado Plateau began to uplift.

The dark-colored vertical stripes often seen on sandstone cliff faces across the Colorado Plateau are known as **desert varnish.** They're mostly composed of very fine clay particles, rich in iron and manganese. It's not entirely known how these streaks are formed, but it seems likely that they're at least partly created by mineral-rich water coursing down the cliffs along the varnished areas and wind-blown clay dust sticking to cliff faces. Bacteria and fungi on the rock's surface may help this process along by absorbing manganese and iron from the atmosphere and precipitating it as a black layer of manganese oxide or reddish iron oxide on the rock surfaces. The clay particles in this thin layer of varnish help shield the bacteria against the drying effects of the desert sun. Prehistoric rock artists worked with desert varnish, chipping away the dark surface to expose the lighter underlying rocks.

WHERE TO SEE COLORFUL ROCKS

- **Red Rocks:** Altar of Sacrifice (page 55)

- **Gray or Brown Rocks:** Grand Staircase (page 103)

- **White Rocks:** Great White Throne (page 60), Checkerboard Mesa (page 62)

- **Pink Rocks:** Hoodoos in Bryce Amphitheater (page 98)

- **Desert Varnish:** Zion Canyon (page 53), Kolob Canyons (page 62)

Great White Throne (top); colorful layers of exposed rock (middle); Altar of Sacrifice in Zion (bottom)

CANYONS

Though much of southwest Utah is arid and desert-like, streams and rivers have worked for millions of years to carve deep canyons in the underlying sandstone and limestone. Because there's little vegetation on the canyon walls, it's easy to see the many layers of sandstone and marine sediments that make up the area's bedrock. By the way, even though it's called Bryce Canyon, the main feature in that park is not a canyon but a vast eroded amphitheater filled with multicolored hoodoos.

WHERE TO SEE CANYONS

- Hidden Canyon Trail (page 70)
- The Narrows (page 71)
- Navajo Loop Trail (page 106)

hikers on a rock staircase along the Hidden Canyon Trail (left); Navajo Loop Trail (right)

the Narrows

the Narrows in Zion

ESSENTIALS

GETTING THERE

AIR

Many tours of Utah's national parks begin in Salt Lake City. Its busy airport and plethora of hotels make it an easy place to begin and end a trip. However, it's smart to consider flying into McCarran International Airport in Las Vegas instead. Not only is it closer to Zion and Bryce, but car rentals are usually about $100 a week cheaper.

Although it may not seem intuitive to start your tour of Utah's national parks in Denver, that's exactly what works best for many folks, especially those who fly from European capital cities to Denver International Airport. From there, it's easy to rent a car or RV and begin a tour that typically includes Rocky Mountain National Park, Utah's five national parks, and the Grand Canyon before terminating at Las Vegas.

Salt Lake City International Airport

SLC; 776 N. Terminal Dr.; 801/575-2400; www.slcairport.com
DRIVING TIME TO ZION: 4.5 hours, mostly along I-15 South
DRIVING TIME TO BRYCE: 4 hours, mostly along I-15 South

McCarran International Airport (Las Vegas)

LAS; 5757 Wayne Newton Blvd.; 702/261-5743; www.mccarran.com
DRIVING TIME TO ZION: 3 hours, mostly along I-15 North
DRIVING TIME TO BRYCE: 4 hours, mostly along I-15 North

Denver International Airport

DEN; 8500 Peña Blvd.; 303/342-2000; www.flydenver.com
DRIVING TIME TO ZION: 10.5 hours, mostly along I-70 West
DRIVING TIME TO BRYCE: 9.5 hours, mostly along I-70 West

BUS

Greyhound buses stop in **Salt Lake City** (160 W. South Temple St.; 801/355-9579 or 800/231-2222; www.greyhound.com) and Las Vegas (220 S. Main St.; 702/383-9792; www.greyhound.com). Generally speaking, buses run north and south along I-15 and east and west along I-80. However, you won't be able to take the bus to any of Utah's national parks.

CAR

To get to Zion and Bryce from Salt Lake City, simply take I-15 south; driving time is about 4.5 hours.

From Las Vegas, it's just 120 miles (193 km) northeast on I-15 to St. George, with Zion just 43 miles (69 km) farther. From Denver, follow I-70 west, up over the Continental Divide along the Rocky Mountains, and down to the Colorado River.

GETTING AROUND

For most travelers, getting around Southern Utah requires using some form of automobile. Public transportation is nonexistent between the parks, and distances are great—although the parks cover a relatively compact area, the geography of the land is so contorted that there are few roads that connect the dots. Cars are easily rented in gateway cities.

TRAVELING BY RV

Traveling the Southwest's national parks in an RV is a time-honored tradition, and travelers will have no problem finding RV rentals in major cities like Denver, Salt Lake City, and Las Vegas, which serve as gateways to the parks of Southern Utah. The parks have good campgrounds, and towns like Springdale have some very spiffy campground options with extras like swimming pools and fine-dining cookouts. Note that some parks limit RV access—during high season, no vehicles are allowed in Zion, where shuttle buses have replaced private vehicles along the scenic Zion Canyon Road. In Bryce, vehicles measuring 20 feet (6 m) or longer are restricted from the Bryce Amphitheater area during shuttle hours.

DRIVING THE PARKS

During the summer, patience is the key to driving in Utah's national parks. Roads are often crowded with slow-moving RVs, and traffic jams are not uncommon.

If you're traveling on back roads, make sure you have plenty of gas, even if it means paying top dollar at a small-town gas pump.

Summer heat in the desert puts an extra strain on both cars and drivers. It's worth double-checking your vehicle's cooling system, engine oil, transmission fluid, fan belts, and tires to make sure they are in top condition. Carry several gallons of water in case of a breakdown or radiator trouble. Never leave children or pets in a parked car during warm weather; temperatures inside can cause fatal heatstroke in minutes.

At times the desert has too much water, when late-summer storms frequently flood low spots in the road. Wait for the water level to subside before crossing. Dust storms can completely block visibility but tend to be short-lived. During such storms, pull completely off the road, stop, and turn off your lights so as not to confuse other drivers. Radio stations carry frequent weather updates when weather hazards exist.

If stranded, stay with your vehicle unless you're positive of where to go for help, then leave a note explaining your route and departure time. Airplanes can easily spot a stranded car (tie a piece of cloth to your antenna), but a person walking is more difficult to see. It's best to carry emergency supplies: blankets or sleeping bags, a first-aid kit, tools, jumper cables, a shovel, traction mats or chains, a flashlight, rain gear, water, food, and a can opener.

Maps

The Utah Department of Transportation prints and distributes a free, regularly updated map of Utah. Ask for it when you call for information or when you stop at a visitor information office. Benchmark Maps' *Utah Road and Recreation Atlas* is loaded with beautiful maps, recreation information, and global positioning system (GPS) grids. If you're planning on extensive backcountry exploration, be sure to ask locally about conditions.

If you're looking for USGS topo maps, you can download them for free at www.topozone.com.

Off-Road Driving

Here are some tips for safely traversing the backcountry in a vehicle (preferably one with four-wheel drive):

- Drive slowly enough to choose a safe path and avoid obstacles such as rocks or giant potholes, but keep up enough speed to propel yourself through sand or mud.

- Keep an eye on the route ahead of you. If there are obstacles, stop, get out of your vehicle, and survey the situation.

- Reduce the tire pressure if you're driving across sand.

- Drive directly up or down the fall line of a slope. Cutting across diagonally may seem less frightening, but it puts you in a position to slide or roll over.

If you really want to learn to drive your 4WD rig, consider signing up for a class.

Charging Your Electric Car

Electric vehicle (EV) charging stations are present in some areas of Southern Utah, but if you plan to explore far-flung destinations, a little preplanning is in order. At press time, EV charging stations are available at St. George, Cedar City, Springdale, the visitor center at Zion National Park, and Ruby's Inn (near Bryce Canyon National Park). That leaves big areas of southeast Utah with no EV charging services.

SHUTTLES

Both Zion and Bryce Canyon National Parks offer shuttle bus service during peak seasons along their primary entrance roads to reduce traffic and vehicular impact on the parks. In Zion, shuttles pick up visitors at various points around Springdale and take them to the park gate, where another shuttle runs park visitors up Zion Canyon Road, stopping at trailheads, scenic overlooks, and Zion Lodge. Essentially, private cars are no longer allowed on Zion Canyon Road during peak season. (Registered overnight guests at Zion Lodge can drive their own vehicles to the hotel.)

In Bryce, the shuttle bus picks up visitors at the park gate and drives the length of the main parkway, making stops at all the major trailheads and vista points in addition to campgrounds, Ruby's Inn, and the Lodge at Bryce Canyon. Using the shuttle bus is not required in Bryce, unless your vehicle is 20 feet (6 m) or longer and you're visiting the Bryce Amphitheater, although it is highly recommended.

In both parks, the shuttle ticket cost is covered by park entrance fees.

TOURS

Bus tours of the Southern Utah national parks, often in conjunction with Grand Canyon National Park, are available from several regional tour companies. **Southern Utah Scenic Tours** (435/656-1504 or 888/404-8687; http://utahscenictours.com) offers multiday scenic and thematic tours of the Southwest, including the Utah national parks.

Road Scholar (800/454-5768; www.roadscholar.org) operates programs out of St. George, including a bus tour of Southern Utah. These trips are geared toward older adults (this is the organization formerly known as Elderhostel) and involve a bit of easy hiking.

For a truly unusual bus tour, consider the **Adventure Bus** (375 S. Main St., Moab; 909/633-7225 or 888/737-5263; www.adventurebus.com), a bus that's had most of its seats removed to make lounge and sleeping areas. Guests live on the bus (some meals are provided) as it makes tours of Utah and other Southwest hot spots.

STREET NUMBERING AND GRID ADDRESSES

Many towns founded by Mormon settlers share a street-numbering scheme that can be confusing to first-time visitors but quickly becomes intuitive. A city's address grid will generally have its temple at the center, with blocks numbered by hundreds out in every direction. For instance, 100 West is one block west of the center of town, then comes 200 West, and so on. In conversation, you may hear the shorthand "4th South," "3rd West," and so on to indicate 400 South or 300 West.

While this street-numbering system is a picture of precision, it's also confusing at first. All addresses have four parts: When you see the address 436 North 100 West, for instance, the system tells you that the address will be found four blocks north of the center of town, on 100 West. One rule of thumb is to remember that the last two segments of an address (300 South, 500 East, 2300 West) are the street's actual name—the equivalent of a single street signifier such as Oak Street or Front Avenue.

NEARBY TOWNS
NEAR ZION
Springdale
With its location just outside Zion's south entrance, Springdale (population 650) is geared toward serving park visitors. Its many high-quality motels and B&Bs, as well as frequent free shuttle bus service to the park's entrance, make Springdale an appealing base for a visit to Zion.

FOOD
There are a number of food options in Springdale, including **Cafe Soleil** (205 Zion Park Blvd.; 435/772-0505; www. cafesoleilzionpark.com; 6am-9pm daily spring-fall, 7am-8pm winter; $8-12), a bright, friendly place for breakfast or a lunchtime sandwich that is a short walk from the park entrance. Springdale's sole brewpub is the **Zion Canyon Brew Pub** (95 Zion Park Blvd.; 435/772-0036; www.zionbrewery.com; 11:30am-10pm daily; $13-29), right at the pedestrian gate to the park.

    King's Landing Bistro (1515 Zion Park Blvd.; 435/772-7422; www.klbzion. com; 5pm-9:30 Mon.-Sat.; $18-30), located at the Driftwood Lodge, serves some of Springdale's most innovative dinners. The town's only full-fledged supermarket, **Sol Foods** (995 Zion Park Blvd.; 435/772-3100; www.solfoods. com; 7am-11pm daily), stocks groceries, deli items, hardware, and camping supplies.

St. George
Southern Utah's largest city, St. George (pop. 93,000) sits between lazy bends of the Virgin River and rocky hills of red sandstone. The city itself will have limited appeal to most park travelers; if your focus is Zion, you'll most likely just use St. George as a jumping-off point. However, St. George's abundance of hotels, a clutch of good restaurants, public art and galleries in the old downtown core, and slickrock-laden state park a few miles away make it a handy place to begin or end your Utah parks adventure.

Cedar City
Cedar City (population about 33,000), known for its scenic setting and its summertime Utah Shakespeare Festival, is a handy base for exploring a good chunk of Southern Utah. Zion National Park's Kolob Canyons area is less than 20 miles (32 km) from Cedar City. Within an easy day's drive are the Zion Canyon section of the park to the south and Bryce Canyon National Park.

NEAR BRYCE
Tropic
Tropic is 11 miles (17.7 km) east of Bryce Canyon National Park on Highway 12, and is visible from many of the park's viewpoints. Travelers think of Tropic primarily for its cache of motels lining Main Street (Hwy. 12), but several pleasant B&Bs also grace the town. There are a few dining options in town.

Panguitch
Panguitch is one of the more pleasant towns in this part of Utah, and it has an abundance of reasonably priced motels, plus a couple of good places to eat. It's a convenient stopover on the road between Zion and Bryce Canyon National Parks.

    Panguitch is on U.S. 89, 7 miles (11.3 km) north of Bryce Junction (Hwy. 12 and U.S. 89). From Bryce Junction, it is 11 miles (17.7 km) east on Highway 12 to Bryce Canyon National Park.

RECREATION
Utah's national parks are home to epic landscapes—red-rock canyons, towering arches, and needles of sandstone that are best explored by foot, by bike, or on the water. Hikers will find a variety of trails, ranging from paved all-abilities paths to remote backcountry tracks. Rafts and jet boats out of Moab provide another means to explore rugged canyons otherwise inaccessible to all but the hardiest trekkers. The sheer rock cliff faces and promontories in the parks provide abundant challenges to experienced rock climbers; be certain to

check park regulations before climbing, however, as restrictions may apply.

HIKING

Utah's national parks offer lots of opportunities for hikers and backcountry enthusiasts interested in exploring the scenery on foot. Each of the parks has a variety of well-maintained hiking trails, ranging from easy strolls to multi-day backcountry treks. In fact, the most compelling parts Zion are accessible only by foot.

One popular activity is canyoneering—exploring mazelike slot canyons. Hundreds of feet deep but sometimes only wide enough for a hiker to squeeze through, these canyons are located across Southern Utah. You'll need to be fit to explore these regions—and watch the weather carefully for flash floods.

CAMPING

All of Utah's national parks have campgrounds, with each park keeping at least one campground open year-round. Some campgrounds are first come, first served; reservations (877/444-6777; www.recreation.gov; reservation fee $9 online, $10 phone) are accepted seasonally at Zion's Watchman Campground and Bryce's Sunset Campground,. During the summer and on holiday weekends during the spring and fall, it's best to arrive at the park early in the day and select a campsite immediately. Don't expect to find hookups or showers at National Park Service campgrounds. For these comforts, look just outside the park entrance, where you'll generally find at least one full-service commercial campground.

Backcountry Camping

Backcountry campers in national parks must stop by the park visitor center for a backcountry permit. Backcountry camping may be limited to specific sites in order to spread people out a bit; if so, a park ranger will consult with you and assign you a campground.

Before heading into the backcountry, check with a ranger about weather, water sources, fire danger, trail conditions, and regulations. Backpacking stores are also good sources of information. Here are some tips for traveling safely and respectfully in the backcountry:

- Tell rangers or other reliable people where you are going and when you expect to return; they'll alert rescuers if you go missing.

- Travel in small groups for the best experience (group size may also be regulated).

- Avoid stepping on—or camping on—fragile cryptobiotic soils.

- Use a portable stove to avoid leaving fire scars.

- Resist the temptation to shortcut switchbacks; this causes erosion and can be dangerous.

- Avoid digging tent trenches or cutting vegetation.

- Help preserve old Native American and other historic ruins.

- Camp at least 300 feet (91 m) away from springs, creeks, and trails. Camp at least 0.25 mile (0.4 km) from a lone water source to avoid scaring away wildlife and livestock.

- Avoid camping in washes at any time; be alert to thunderstorms.

- Take care not to throw or kick rocks off trails—someone might be below you.

- Don't drink water directly from streams or lakes, no matter how clean the water appears; it may contain the parasitic protozoan Giardia lamblia, which causes giardiasis. Boiling water for several minutes

THE AMERICA THE BEAUTIFUL PASS

The U.S. government has revamped its park pass system, inaugurating a new set of annual passes that are the result of a cooperative effort between the National Park Service, the U.S. Forest Service, the U.S. Fish and Wildlife Service, the Bureau of Land Management, and the Bureau of Reclamation.

The **basic pass** is called the America the Beautiful—National Parks and Federal Recreational Lands Pass (valid for 1 year from date of purchase; $80 plus a $5 processing and handling fee), which is available to the general public and provides access to, and use of, federal recreation sites that charge an entrance or standard amenity fee. Passes can be obtained in person at a park; by calling 888/ASK-USGS (888/275-8747, ext. 1); or at http://store.usgs.gov/pass.

U.S. citizens or permanent residents age 62 or older can purchase a **lifetime version** of the America the Beautiful pass for $80. This pass can only be obtained in person at a park. The Senior Pass provides free access to federal parks and recreational areas, plus a 50 percent discount on some fees, such as camping, swimming, boat launch, and specialized interpretive services.

Both passes are good for the cardholder plus three adults (children 15 and under are free). The pass is nontransferable and generally does not cover or reduce special recreation permit fees or fees charged by park concessionaires.

U.S. citizens or permanent residents with permanent disabilities are eligible for a free lifetime **America the Beautiful Access Pass.** Documentation such as a statement from a licensed physician, the Veterans Administration, or Social Security is required to obtain this pass, which can only be obtained in person at a park. Like the Senior Pass, the Access Pass provides free access to federal parks and recreational areas, plus a 50 percent discount on some fees, such as camping, swimming, boat launch, and specialized interpretive services. Free annual passes are also available to members of the U.S. military and their families.

Volunteers who have amassed 250 service hours with one of the participating federal agencies are eligible for a **free one-year pass,** which is available through their supervisor.

will kill giardia as well as most other bacterial or viral pathogens. Chemical treatments and water filters usually work too, although they're not as reliable as boiling (giardia spends part of its life in a hard shell that protects it from most chemicals).

- Bathe and wash dishes away from lakes, streams, and springs. Use biodegradable soap, and scatter your wash water.

- Bring a trowel for personal sanitation. Dig 6-8 inches (15-20 cm) deep and cover your waste; in some areas, you'll be required to carry portable human waste disposal systems.

- Pack out all your trash, including toilet paper and feminine hygiene items.

- Bring plenty of feed for your horses and mules.

- Leave dogs at home; they're not permitted on national park trails.

- If you realize you're lost, find shelter. If you're sure of a way to civilization and plan to walk out, leave a note with your departure time and planned route.

- Visit the Leave No Trace website (www.lnt.org) for more details on responsible backcountry travel.

CLIMBING

Most visitors to Utah's national parks enjoy spotting rock climbers scaling canyon walls and sandstone pillars, but for a few, the whole reason to visit Southern Utah is to climb. These folks need a climbing guide, either the classic *Desert Rock* by Eric Bjørnstad or *Rock Climbing Utah* by Stewart M. Green.

Prospective climbers should take note: Just because you're the star of the local rock gym, don't think that climbing Zion's high, exposed big walls is going to be simple. Sandstone poses its own set of challenges; it weakens when wet, so it's wise to avoid climbing in damp areas or after rain.

Climbers in the national parks should take care to use clean climbing techniques. Approach climbs via established trails to prevent further erosion of slopes. Camp in park campgrounds or, on multiday climbs, get a backcountry permit. Because white chalk leaves unsightly marks on canyon walls, add red pigment to your chalk.

Do not disturb vegetation growing in cracks along your route. Tube or bag human waste and carry it out. Remove all old worn rope and equipment, but do not remove fixed pins. Make sure your climb is adequately protected by visually inspecting any preexisting bolts or fixed pins. It is illegal to use a power drill to place bolts. Never climb directly above trails, where hikers may be hit by dislodged rocks.

Plan to climb in the spring or fall. During the summer, the walls become extremely hot. Some climbing areas may be closed during the spring to protect nesting raptors. Check at the visitor centers for current closures.

RANGER PROGRAMS
ZION

Except for ranger-led walks, classes organized by Zion National Park Forever, horseback rides from Zion Lodge, and the running commentary from the more loquacious shuttle-bus drivers, Zion is a do-it-yourself park. Outfitters are not permitted to lead trips within the park. If you'd like a guided tour outside park boundaries, where you'll find equally stunning scenery and adventure, several outfitters in Springdale lead cycling, canyoneering, and climbing trips.

The best way to get a feel for Zion's impressive geology and variety of habitats is to take in a talk of walk with a park ranger. Many nature programs and hikes are offered late March-November; check the posted schedule at the Zion Canyon Visitor Center. Children's programs, including the popular Junior Ranger program, are held intermittently during March and April and daily Memorial Day-mid-August at Zion Nature Center near South Campground; ask at the visitor center for details.

Zion National Park Forever (435/772-3264; https://zionpark.org) is authorized to run educational programs in the park, which include animal tracking, photography, and archaeology; fees vary.

DARK SKIES

Bryce Canyon National Park, sky-high and far from sources of light pollution, is recognized as an **International Dark Sky Park,** and the stars here really do pop out of the night sky. Astronomy buffs should plan to visit in mid-June, when the park holds a four-day **Astronomy Festival,** with guest speakers, workshops, and constellation "tours."

More casual guided stargazing is possible several times a week during the summer when rangers lead **astronomy programs,** usually with a telescope on hand, at the visitor center. If you really want to get the stars in your eyes, plan to visit around the new moon, when skies are darkest. On the other hand, full-moon nights often bring a chance to take a ranger-led **moonlit hike.**

On your own, head out to **Yovimpa Point** to get a look at the Milky Way or view the mid-August Perseid meteor showers. But do make sure to bring a proper flashlight to make your way back to your car!

Although Zion's night sky is not as celebrated, a nighttime walk along the **Pa'rus Trail,** with the rock cliffs etched against the sky, is certainly beautiful. Even better views come from the **Kolob Terrace** or **Kolob Canyons** areas, both of which are outside deep Zion Canyon.

Bryce Canyon at night during the Astronomy Festival

BRYCE

Rangers offer daily Geology Talks or Rim Walks throughout the year, and twice daily from Memorial Day through September. Evening programs that focus on park natural history or other topics take place every evening during summer either at the Lodge Auditorium or the North Campground Amphitheater. In addition, during summer months when conditions are right, rangers also offer "star parties" that explore the night sky, along with the opportunity to use telescopes to gaze at distant galaxies. You can also join one of Bryce Canyon's "Night Sky Rangers" for a Full Moon Hike, offered only during the full moon. In winter, when snowfall allows, rangers also lead Snowshoe Hikes (snowshoes provided) that explore the winter ecology of the park.

For information on ranger-led programs check out the listings on the park website (www.nps.gov/brca/planyourvisit/ranger-programs.htm) or look at the list posted at the visitor center.

ACCESSIBILITY

Travelers with disabilities will find Utah progressive when it comes to accessibility. Both Zion and Bryce Canyon National Parks have all-abilities trails and services. Both national parks have reasonably good facilities for visitors with limited mobility. Visitor centers are all accessible, and at least a couple of trails in each park are paved or smooth enough for wheelchair users to navigate with some assistance. Each park has a few accessible campsites.

Most hotels also offer some form of barrier-free lodging. It's best to call ahead and inquire what these accommodations are, however, because these services can vary quite a bit from one establishment to another.

TRAVELING WITH PETS

Unless you really have no other option, it's best not to bring your dog (or cat, or bird, or ferret) along on a national park vacation. Although pets are allowed in national parks, they aren't permitted on the trails. This limits you and your dog to leashed walks along the roads, around campground loops, and in parking areas. During much of the year, it's far too hot to leave an animal in a parked car.

In Zion, private cars are prohibited on the scenic canyon drive, and no pets are allowed on the shuttle buses that drive this route. Pet boarding is available just outside Zion at the **Doggy Dude Ranch** (800 E. Main St, Rockville; 435/772-3105; www.doggyduderanch.com).

HEALTH AND SAFETY

There's nothing inherently dangerous about Utah's national parks, though a few precautions can help minimize what risks do exist. For the most part, using common sense about the dangers of extreme temperatures, remote backcountry exploration, and encounters with wildlife will ensure a safe and healthy trip.

HEAT AND WATER

Southern Utah in summer is a very hot place. Be sure to use sunscreen, or else you risk having an uncomfortable vacation. Wearing a wide-brimmed hat and good sunglasses, with full UV protection, can shield you from the sun's harmful effects. Heat exhaustion can also be a problem if you're hiking in the hot sun. In midsummer, try to get an early start if you're hiking in full sun. If you're out during the heat of the afternoon, look for a shady spot and rest until the sun begins to drop.

Drink steadily throughout the day, whether you are thirsty or not, rather than gulping huge amounts of water once you feel thirsty. For hikers, one of the best ways to drink enough is to carry water in a hydration pack (the two top brands are CamelBak and Platypus). These collapsible plastic bladders come with a hose and a mouthpiece, so you can carry your water in your pack, threading the hose out the top of the pack and over your shoulder, which keeps the mouthpiece handy for frequent sips of water. One easy way to tell if you're getting enough to drink is to monitor your urine output. If you're only urinating a couple of times a day, and the color and odor of your urine are both strong, it's time to start drinking more water.

HYPOTHERMIA

Don't think that just because you're in the Utah desert that you're immune to hypothermia. This lowering of the body's temperature below 95°F (35°C) causes disorientation, uncontrollable shivering, slurred speech, and drowsiness. The victim may not even realize what's wrong. Unless corrective action is taken immediately, hypothermia can lead to death. Hikers should therefore travel with companions and always carry wind and rain protection. Space blankets are lightweight and cheap and offer protection against the cold in emergencies. Remember that temperatures can plummet rapidly in Utah's dry climate—a drop of 40 degrees between day and night is common. Be especially careful at high elevations, where sunshine can quickly change into freezing rain or a blizzard. Simply falling into a mountain stream can also lead to hypothermia and death unless proper action is taken. If you're cold and tired, don't waste time: Seek shelter and build a fire, change into dry clothes, and drink warm liquids. If a victim isn't fully conscious, warm him or her by skin-to-skin contact in a sleeping bag. Try to keep the victim awake and offer plenty of warm liquids.

GIARDIA

Giardia lamblia is a protozoan that has become common in even the remotest mountain streams. It is carried in animal or human waste that is deposited or washed into the water. When ingested, it begins reproducing, causing intense cramping and diarrhea in the host; this can become serious and may require medical attention.

No matter how clear a stream looks, it's best to assume that it is contaminated and to take precautions against giardia by filtering, boiling, or treating water with chemicals before drinking it. A high-quality filter will remove giardia and a host of other things you don't want to be drinking. (Spend a bit extra for one that removes particles down to one micrometer in size.) It's also effective to simply boil your water; two to five minutes at a rolling boil will kill giardia even in the cyst stage. Because water boils at a lower temperature as elevation increases, increase the boiling time to 15 minutes if you're at 9,000 feet (2,743 m). Two drops of bleach left in a quart of water for 30 minutes will remove most giardia, although some microorganisms are resistant to chemicals.

HANTAVIRUS

Hantavirus is an infectious disease agent that was first isolated during the Korean War and then discovered in the Americas in 1993 by a task force of scientists in New Mexico. This disease agent occurs naturally throughout most of North and South America, especially in dry desert conditions. The infectious agent is airborne, and in the absence of prompt medical attention, its infections are usually fatal. This disease is called hantavirus pulmonary syndrome (HPS). It can affect anyone, but given some fundamental knowledge, it can also easily be prevented.

The natural host of the hantavirus appears to be rodents, especially mice and rats. The virus is not usually transmitted directly from rodents to humans; rather, the rodents shed hantavirus particles in their saliva, urine, and droppings. Humans usually contract HPS by inhaling particles that are infected with the hantavirus. The virus becomes airborne when the particles dry out and get stirred into the air (especially from sweeping a floor or shaking a rug). Humans then inhale these particles, which leads to the infection.

HPS is not considered a highly infectious disease, so people usually contract HPS from long-term exposure. Because transmission usually occurs through inhalation, it is easiest for a human being to contract hantavirus within a contained environment, where the virus-infected particles are not thoroughly dispersed. Being in a cabin or barn where rodents can be found poses elevated risks for contracting the infection.

Simply traveling to a place where the hantavirus is known to occur is not considered a risk factor. Camping, hiking, and other outdoor activities also pose low risk, especially if steps are taken to reduce rodent contact. If you happen to stay in a rodent-infested cabin, thoroughly wet any droppings and dead rodents with a chlorine bleach solution (one cup of bleach per gallon of water) and let them stand for a few minutes before cleaning them up. Be sure to wear rubber gloves for this task, and double-bag your garbage.

The first symptoms of HPS can occur anywhere between five days and three weeks after infection. They almost always include fever, fatigue, aching muscles (usually in the back, shoulders, or thighs), and other flu-like symptoms. Other early symptoms may include headaches, dizziness, chills, and abdominal discomfort such as vomiting, nausea, or diarrhea. These symptoms are shortly followed by intense coughing and shortness of breath. If you have these symptoms, seek medical help immediately. Untreated infections of hantavirus are almost always fatal.

FLASH FLOODS

Rainwater runs quickly off the rocky desert surfaces and into gullies and canyons. A summer thunderstorm or a rapid late-winter snowmelt can send torrents of mud and boulders rumbling down dry washes and canyons. Backcountry drivers, horseback riders, and hikers need to avoid hazardous locations when storms threaten or unseasonably warm winds blow on the winter snowpack.

Flash floods can sweep away anything in their path, including boulders, cars, and campsites. Do not camp or park in potential flash flood areas. If you come to a section of flooded roadway—a common occurrence on desert roads after storms—wait until the water goes down before crossing (it shouldn't take long). Summer lightning causes forest and brush fires, posing a danger to hikers who are foolish enough to climb mountains when storms threaten.

The bare rock and loose soils so common in the canyon country do little to hold back the flow of rain or meltwater. In fact, slickrock is effective at shedding water as fast as it comes in contact. Logs and other debris wedged high on canyon walls give proof enough of past floods.

THINGS THAT BITE OR STING

Although travelers in Utah's national parks are not going to get attacked by a grizzly bear, and encounters with mountain lions are rare, there are a few animals to watch out for. Snakes, scorpions, and spiders are all present in considerable numbers, and there are a few key things to know about dealing with this phobia-inducing trio.

Snakes

Rattlesnakes, including the particularly venomous midget faded rattlesnake, are present throughout Southern Utah. The midget faded snakes frequent

MOUNTAIN LION ENCOUNTERS

Imagine hiking down a trail and suddenly noticing fresh large paw prints. Mountain lion or Labrador retriever? Here's the way to tell the difference: Mountain lions usually retract their claws when they walk. Dogs, of course, can't do this. So if close inspection of the print reveals toenails, it's most likely from a canine's paw.

But about those mountain lions: In recent years, incidents of mountain lion-human confrontations have increased markedly and received much publicity. These ambush hunters usually prey on sick or weak animals but will occasionally attack people, especially children and small adults. When hiking or camping with children in mountain lion territory—potentially all of Utah's national parks—it is important to keep them close to the rest of the family.

If you are stalked by a mountain lion, make yourself look big by raising your arms, waving a big stick, or spreading your coat. Maintain direct eye contact with the animal, and do not turn your back to it. If the mountain lion begins to approach, throw rocks and sticks, and continue to look large and menacing as you slowly back away. In the case of an attack, fight back; do not "play dead."

To put things in perspective, it's important to remember that mountain lions are famously elusive. If you do see one, it will probably be a quick glimpse of the cat running away from you.

burrows and rock crevices and are mostly active at night. Even though their venom is toxic, full venom injections are relatively uncommon, and, like all rattlesnakes, they pose little threat unless they're provoked.

If you see a rattlesnake, observe it at a safe distance. Be careful where you put your hands when canyoneering or scrambling—it's not a good idea to reach above your head and blindly plant your hands on a sunny rock ledge. Hikers should wear sturdy boots to minimize the chance that a snake's fangs will reach the skin if a bite occurs. Do not walk barefoot outside after dark, as this is when snakes hunt for prey.

First aid for rattlesnake bites is full of conflicting ideas: to suck or not to suck; to apply a constricting bandage or not; to take time treating in the field versus rushing to the hospital. Most people who receive medical treatment after being bitten by a rattlesnake live to tell the story. Prompt administration of antivenin is the most important treatment, and the most important aspect of first aid is to arrange transportation of the victim to a hospital as quickly as possible.

Scorpions

A scorpion's sting isn't as painful as you'd expect (it's about like a bee sting), and the venom is insufficient to cause any real harm. Still, it's not what you'd call pleasant, and experienced desert campers know to shake out their boots every morning, as scorpions and spiders are attracted to warm, moist, dark places.

Spiders

Tarantulas and black widow spiders are present across much of the Colorado Plateau. Believe it or not, a tarantula's

CORONAVIRUS IN ZION & BRYCE

At the time of writing, Utah was managing the effects of the coronavirus, with the situation constantly evolving. Most, if not all, destinations required that **face masks** be worn in enclosed spaces, and **social distancing** was encouraged. As Utah's Department of Health monitors COVID-19 cases and transmission through the state, phased guidelines may change locally, so check the websites below regularly. The National Park Service also emphasizes the importance of park visitors wearing masks

Now more than ever, Moon encourages its readers to be courteous and ethical in their travel. We ask travelers to be respectful to residents, and mindful of the evolving situation in their chosen destination when planning their trip.

Before You Go

Check relevant websites (listed below) for **updated local restrictions** and the overall health status of the destination.

- If you plan to fly, check with your **airline** and the **local health authorities** for updated recommendation requirements.
- Check the website of any venues you wish to patronize to confirm that they're open, if their hours have been adjusted,

bite does not poison humans; the enzymes secreted when they bite turn the insides of frogs, lizards, and insects to a soft mush, allowing the tarantula to suck the guts from its prey. Another interesting tarantula fact: While males live about as long as you'd expect a spider to live, female tarantulas can live for up to 25 years. Females do sometimes eat the males, which may account for some of this disparity in longevity.

Black widow spiders, on the other hand, have a toxic bite. Although the bite is usually painless, it delivers a potent neurotoxin, which quickly causes pain, nausea, and vomiting. It is important to seek immediate treatment for a black widow bite; although few people actually die from these bites, recovery is helped along considerably by antivenin.

RESOURCES

The American Southwest
www.americansouthwest.net/utah
This online Utah guide provides an overview of national parks, national recreation areas, and some state parks.

Desert USA
www.desertusa.com
Desert USA's Utah section discusses places to visit and what plants and animals you might meet there. Here's the best part of this site: You can find out what's in bloom at www.desertusa.com/wildflo/nv.html.

National Park Service
www.nps.gov
The National Park Service offers pages for all its units at this site. You can also enter this address followed by a slash and the first two letters of the first two

and to learn about any specific visitation requirements, such as mandatory reservations.
- Pack **hand sanitizer, a thermometer,** and plenty of **face masks.** Road trippers may want to bring a **cooler** to limit the number of stops along their route.
- Assess the risk of entering **crowded spaces,** joining **tours,** and taking **public transit.**
- Expect **general disruptions.** Events may be postponed or cancelled. Some tours and venues may require reservations, enforce limits on the number of guests, or operate during different hours than the ones listed. Some may be closed entirely. In the parks, the number of riders on **park shuttles** may be restricted, and shuttles may operate under reduced schedules.

Resources

Monitor the following websites to keep track of the evolving COVID-19 situation in Utah.
- **Utah Health Department:** https://coronavirus.utah.gov
- **Utah State Travel Bureau:** www.visitutah.com/plan-your-trip/covid-19
- **National Park Service:** www.nps.gov/planyourvisit/alerts.htm

words of the place (first four letters if there's just a one-word name); for example, www.nps.gov/brca takes you to Bryce Canyon National Park and www.nps.gov/zion leads to Zion National Park.

Recreation.gov

www.recreation.gov
If a campground is operated by the federal government, this is the place to make a reservation. You can expect to pay close to $10 for this convenience.

Reserve America

www.reserveamerica.com
Use this website to reserve campsites in state campgrounds. It costs a few extra bucks to reserve a campsite, but compare that with the cost of being skunked out of a site and having to resort to a motel room.

Greater Zion

www.utahsdixie.com
The southwestern Utah city of St. George is the focus of this site, which also covers some of the smaller communities outside Zion National Park.

Utah Travel Council

https://utah.com
The Utah Travel Council is a one-stop shop for all sorts of information on Utah. It takes you around the state to sights, activities, events, and maps, and offers links to local tourism offices. The accommodations listings are the most up-to-date source for current room rates and options.

Zion Park

www.zionpark.com

This site will point you to information on Springdale and the area surrounding Zion National Park, with links to lodging and restaurant sites.

Zion National Park Forever

www.zionpark.org

Learn about (and purchase tickets for) upcoming educational programs in Zion National Park.

Ruby's Inn

www.rubysinn.com

Book activities in Bryce Canyon National Park, from ATV tours to horseback rides.

INDEX

LIST OF MAPS

PHOTO CREDITS

MAP SYMBOLS

═══	Highway	○	City/Town	🅿	Parking Area	🛉	Small Park
▭▭▭	Primary Road	◉	State Capital	🆃	Trailhead	▲	Mountain Peak
▭▭▭	Secondary Road	⊛	National Capital	🅱	Bike Trailhead		Unique Natural
⌁⌁⌁	Unpaved Road	★	Top 3 Sight	🅰	Camping	✛	Feature
----------	Trail	(🚶)	Top Hike	🅿	Picnic Area	✛	Unique Hydro Feature
▬▬▬	Paved Trail	★	Highlight/Sight	Ⓜ	Mass Transit		
▭▭▭	Pedestrian Walkway	•	Accommodation	✈	Airport	🗝	Waterfall
⋯⋯⋯	Ferry	▾	Restaurant/Bar	✗	Airfield	🎿	Ski Area
⊶⊶⊶	Railroad	▪	Other Site	🛉	Place of Worship	⬭	Glacier

CONVERSION TABLES

°C = (°F - 32) / 1.8
°F = (°C x 1.8) + 32
1 inch = 2.54 centimeters (cm)
1 foot = 0.304 meters (m)
1 yard = 0.914 meters
1 mile = 1.6093 kilometers (km)
1 km = 0.6214 miles
1 fathom = 1.8288 m
1 chain = 20.1168 m
1 furlong = 201.168 m
1 acre = 0.4047 hectares
1 sq km = 100 hectares
1 sq mile = 2.59 square km
1 ounce = 28.35 grams
1 pound = 0.4536 kilograms
1 short ton = 0.90718 metric ton
1 short ton = 2,000 pounds
1 long ton = 1.016 metric tons
1 long ton = 2,240 pounds
1 metric ton = 1,000 kilograms
1 quart = 0.94635 liters
1 US gallon = 3.7854 liters
1 Imperial gallon = 4.5459 liters
1 nautical mile = 1.852 km

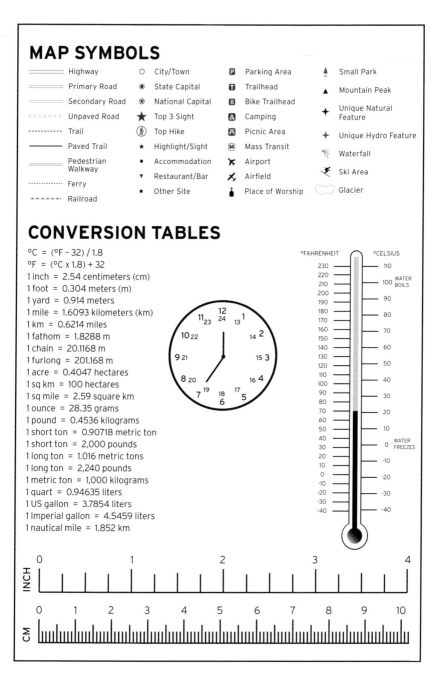

MOON BEST OF ZION & BRYCE
Avalon Travel
Hachette Book Group
1700 Fourth Street
Berkeley, CA 94710, USA
www.moon.com

Editor: Nikki Ioakimedes
Managing Editor: Hannah Brezack
Copy Editor: Kathryn Roque
Production and Graphics Coordinator:
   Lucie Ericksen
Cover Design: Marcie Lawrence
Interior Design: Tabitha Lahr
Moon Logo: Tim McGrath
Map Editor: Mike Morgenfeld
Cartographer: John Culp
Proofreader: Megan Anderluh

ISBN-13: 978-1-64049-526-5

Printing History
1st Edition — May 2021
5 4 3 2 1

Text © 2021 by Judy Jewell and
   W. C. McRae.
Maps © 2021 by Avalon Travel.

Printed in China by RR Donnelley

Avalon Travel is a division of Hachette Book Group, Inc. Moon and the Moon logo are trademarks of Hachette Book Group, Inc. All other marks and logos depicted are the property of the original owners.